APPLES of GOLD

Thomas Malone

APPLES of GOLD

Tom Malone

First Printing: August 2020
20 21 22 23 24 25   10 9 8 7 6 5 4 3 2 1
Printed in the United States of America

Preface

When I wrote the first draft of this book, I had set out the chapters in historical sequential order. By that, I mean, I arranged the chapters in order of when the events in question occurred within the timeline recorded in the gospels. Therefore, the Water Into Wine chapter, depicting the Wedding at Cana, was chapter one because it occurred first. The Road to Emmaus chapter was chapter six because the biblical account of the Emmaus Road episode historically occurred last. I then realised that whilst this might be the natural order to set the chapters in, it is the Road to Emmaus chapter which explains how I came to my personal perspectives and interpretations of all six chapters. It is for that reason that The Road to Emmaus is now chapter one. By presenting it first I hope to demonstrate by its contents that I didn't contrive, strategically develop or formulate any of the teaching or interpretations which I present within the pages of this book. Rather, that through my love for and application of the bible from the time of my conversion and my constant and continual total reliance upon the Holy Spirit to bring the scriptures to life for me, I have at different times and over many years, simply 'received' some spiritual insight and clarity. Insight and clarity which I feel has greatly helped me understand God, life, church, and kingdom and which I have hopefully applied throughout my spiritual walk and service to others.

What I'm trying to say is that I am not a strategic writer of sermons. I don't ever think, "I've got something to say to the church; let me sit down and pull together some scriptures that will fit." What I do is to share what I feel I have received from the Lord, either a specific prompting at the time or, more commonly, from the biblical truths I have learned over my years as a believer. To use just four scriptures to emphasise this: Firstly, Jesus said that every scribe (teacher) brings out of his treasure (the wealth of things he has learned) things old and new. A bible teacher can, when required, draw from what he has previously learned, but also what he may be learning at the time. Hence - things old and things new. Secondly: Jesus said that what we hear in our ear, we should preach that upon the housetops. So, bible teachers and preachers should teach and preach that which they hear from the Lord. Thirdly, Jesus taught that the Comforter, who is the Holy Spirit, would come in his name and lead the believer into all truth and that he (the Holy Spirit) would teach us all things.

Fourth and finally, Paul the Apostle writing in the book of Ephesians, said he prayed that God would give the church a spirit of "wisdom and revelation" concerning the knowledge of God.

What I offer in the following chapters is not something I've made up. It is not something I've figured out by way of pulling lots of scriptures together so they'll somehow sound appealing. The contents of the six chapters and their themes are rather an attempt to convey some of the spiritual truths I have received and been taught by the Holy Spirit and which have been revealed to me. I have been teaching these themes in churches for many years and so far they seem to bless, help, encourage - and at times, challenge others. I humbly hope they might do the same for you.

The very concept of presenting the bible verse "Apples of Gold in Pictures of Silver" as a means of capturing a picture of specific spiritual truth within a contextual frame of particular events in the life and ministry of Jesus, is, I think, quite a brilliant idea. However the idea is not mine. I'm simply not that smart. Many years ago, the "still small voice" of the Holy Spirit whispered it in my ear, told me to use it as a ministry framework, and when I had the time, to write a book on it. I now have the time. Here it is!

Introduction - Apples of Gold

The title of this book is part of a verse in the Authorised King James Bible (AKJV) translation found in Proverbs 25:11. "A word fitly spoken is like apples of gold in pictures of silver."

I should say from the start that my main bible is the Authorised King James Version. This is for a variety of reasons, one of which is I just love its style, it's language and how each verse is set and numbered separately. To avoid using some of the archaic words in the AKJV, and for that reason only, I have used the New King James Version throughout this book - apart from the title verse - because it is the precise wording of that verse which initially, a very long time ago, inspired me to use it for this book's title

"Apples of gold in pictures of silver" depicts a painting of apples made of gold, displayed within a frame made of silver. Gold and silver, the two most precious and pure metals in existence.

The gold apples represent the pure, precious, eternal, life-giving, self-reproducing, and abundantly fruitful treasure of the word of God - The Bible. The frame represents the setting within which the word of God is presented and displayed.

Each picture speaks for itself. It is entirely unique. It is pleasant to look at and is self-contained. It is fixed. It is what it is. It is not complicated. The subject matter is contained within a frame and is self-explanatory. It simply says what it says, and it doesn't change. Everything the picture has to say is contained within the frame. It is complete and will be forever complete. Everything the reader needs to know about the picture is plain to see. It is quite simple. Yet it is also deeply profound.

For example, chapter two: The Wedding at Cana - which gives the account of Jesus turning water into wine, is told in the bible in a mere ten verses. Yet, as I aim to demonstrate, the actual depth of meaning, the breadth of biblical truth, and the height of scriptural revelation contained within those ten short verses are so comprehensive, expansive and profoundly meaningful, that it could take thousands of verses to explain. Yet, it is presented for all the world to see, as a brief snapshot, a picture in place, and time. So, the golden apples are the actual words used in the bible to tell the story and to describe the event. Whilst the silver frame is the context, the place, and the setting in which the story is told.

Each of the six chapters of Apples of Gold similarly seeks to capture and expand on significant biblical events - and the truth they represent - in the life and ministry of Jesus and his early disciples. My hope is that they might serve to illuminate some of the original and early simple and basic truths, both taught - and demonstrated - by Jesus, to his disciples. I earnestly believe that the church today would greatly benefit by revisiting those scenes and re-engaging with what they have to teach us.

I believe Apples of Gold has a valuable contribution to make to Christians everywhere and particularly to fellow pastors and those whose calling and passion is to open up the scriptures to others and, in so doing - feed the flock of God. The offerings within each chapter are not presented as analytical, theoretical, or academic but rather have been applied and tried and tested throughout the many and various chapters of my own life and ministry.

Thomas Malone

Table of Contents

Chapter One

The Road to Emmaus

(The road to revelation and relationship)

Gospel of Luke Chapter 24: Verses 13-35

¹³Now behold, two of them were traveling that same day to a village called Emmaus, which was seven miles from Jerusalem. ¹⁴And they talked together of all these things which had happened. ¹⁵So it was, while they conversed and reasoned, that Jesus Himself drew near and went with them.

¹⁶But their eyes were restrained, so that they did not know Him. ¹⁷And He said to them, "What kind of conversation is this that you have with one another as you walk and are sad?" ¹⁸Then the one whose name was Cleopas answered and said to Him, "Are You the only stranger in Jerusalem, and have You not known the things which happened there in these days?"

¹⁹And He said to them, "What things?" So they said to Him, "The things concerning Jesus of Nazareth, who was a Prophet mighty in deed and word before God and all the people, ²⁰and how the chief priests and our rulers delivered Him to be condemned to death, and crucified Him. ²¹But we were hoping that it was He who was going to redeem Israel. Indeed, besides all this, today is the third day since these things happened.

²²Yes, and certain women of our company, who arrived at the tomb early, astonished us. ²³When they did not find His body, they came *saying that they had also seen a vision of angels who said He was alive. ^{24}And certain of those who were with us went to the tomb and found it just as the women had said; but Him they did not see."*

^{25}Then He said to them, "O foolish ones, and slow of heart to believe in all that the prophets have spoken! ^{26}Ought not the Christ to have suffered these things and to enter into His glory?" ^{27}And beginning at Moses and all the Prophets, He expounded to them in all the Scriptures the things concerning Himself. ^{28}Then they drew near to the village where they were going, and He indicated that He would have gone farther. ^{29}But they constrained Him, saying, "Abide with us, for it is toward evening, and the day is far spent." And He went in to stay with them.

^{30}Now it came to pass, as He sat at the table with them, that He took bread, blessed and broke it, and gave it to them. ^{31}Then their eyes were opened and they knew Him; and He vanished from their sight. ^{32}And they said to one another, "Did not our heart burn within us while He talked with us on the road, and while He opened the Scriptures to us?" ^{33}So they rose up that very hour and returned to Jerusalem, and found the eleven and those who were with them gathered together, ^{34}saying, "The Lord is risen indeed, and has appeared to Simon!" ^{35}And they told about the things that had happened on the road, and how He was known to them in the breaking of bread.

Here is a profoundly significant picture of discipleship. A disciple of Jesus is someone who walks with Jesus, is taught by Jesus, and who is called to emulate Jesus. To be like Jesus and to do the works that Jesus did. This picture will lead us to gradually unfold, then discover just how that truly works in practice. We will discover the truth about how Jesus both taught and trained those who truly draw close to him. The truths contained within this picture, these apples of gold, are contained within the silver frame of a walk. A walk from one place to another. A walk from one destination to another. A walk from one purpose to another.

Just as we each journey through life. Every day having its duties, challenges, tasks, and demands, we are constantly on a journey—the journey of life. But more so, the journey of the Christian life. The Christian life is no ordinary one. A Christian, by definition, is a person who is a follower of Christ. A person who, at some point in their journey through life, has had an encounter with God after hearing the good news, the gospel, and who consequently experienced a dramatic change within themselves that caused them to leave their old life behind them. A life whereby they walked their own way, doing their own will, thinking their own thoughts, and essentially only serving themselves. But after encountering the Christ of the gospel, they now live a new life with a new purpose, new values, and new goals. A life whereby they no longer follow their own path but now follow a path upon which he leads them.

Such were these two disciples, one of whom was called Cleopas. They were walking that day the fairly short distance from Jerusalem to the village of Emmaus. It was the same day that Jesus had earlier risen from the dead, having been crucified and placed in a tomb three days earlier. Whilst they walked, they were talking about these events and "reasoning" or to put it another way, discussing and deliberating, what had taken place. The scriptures say that as they were walking and talking, that Jesus himself joined them and began to walk with them. Of extreme significance is that it says that their eyes were restrained so that they couldn't recognise him.

The very same thing happened earlier that morning when Mary went to the tomb. She saw Jesus but didn't recognise him but thought he was the gardener. It is made clear that these two disciples were somehow and for some reason, being prevented from recognising him. From this and other scriptures related to Jesus after his resurrection, it seems that he did look somehow different than before.

We are not given more details. I feel that it's not the actual reason they didn't know who he was. We discover later that it was more of a spiritual reason than a natural or physical one. Remember, many of Jesus' disciples had spent considerable time, some of them over three years with him, and had last seen him only a few days earlier. They were very familiar with him. From this and other accounts of him engaging with his disciples after his resurrection, it seems clear that there was something different about him. Something about him had changed.

So, as they walked the road, Jesus joined them and immediately asked them what they were talking about, but he particularly asked them why they were so sad. Jesus, of course, must have known precisely what they were talking about. I believe he was challenging them. And that he was doing so in preparation for telling them off, which we discover is exactly what he did. Remember, these two men were still his disciples. Disciples he had been teaching only days earlier. And now, following his resurrection, even though they thought he was dead, he was just carrying on as before. He was simply continuing to - walk - with his disciples whilst personally teaching them along the way. And that, I believe, is precisely the same for the believer today, the 21st-century disciple. The very same resurrected Jesus walks with us today by the presence of his indwelling Spirit.

Furthermore and crucially, he also continues, just like then, to engage with us, to speak personally and directly to us, and to constantly and continually teach us. It must be said - that is if we are listening!

Cleopas' response to Jesus's question is interesting. He seemed annoyed and critical of Jesus, saying in effect - you must be the only one around here who doesn't know what's been going on. He then gave Jesus a blow by blow detailed account of recent events.

Something along the lines of - This is what happened concerning Jesus of Nazareth, then that happened, then he was crucified, but we had been hoping he would do such and such. Then some amongst us went to his tomb this morning but didn't find him but said they saw a vision; then others went to see, and so on. Cleopas' conversation was essentially along the lines of - he said / she said, and we thought, and we were hoping, and she went, but this happened, and that happened, and it's now been three days, etc.

Now I don't mean to seem flippant, critical or unkind - but isn't that just like so much Christian conversation these days? It's all about: events, meetings, what happened, who said what and to whom and so on. Not to mention that so many believers, just like Cleopas, think something should have happened but didn't. Cleopas said - but we were hoping it was he who was going to redeem Israel. Despite the fact that Jesus had consistently taught his disciples over three years, that was not what he came to do. So, it was, in fact, a case of Cleopas and some other disciples who were now disappointed, discouraged, and sad because they thought the Messiah hadn't done something that he never said he was going to do in the first place. Furthermore, they also believed that he hadn't done what he said he would do. Sound familiar?

There was a sense of disappointment, confusion, discouragement, and dismay amongst these early followers of Jesus. Disappointment, confusion, discouragement, and dismay, which was firmly rooted in wrong thinking.

Wrong thinking that was firmly based on a lack of information. A lack of information that was the result of them not having been receptive to Jesus' teaching.

By not having been receptive, I simply mean - they clearly hadn't been listening to what he had been teaching them for three years. Not to mention their evident poor knowledge of the scriptures, which in their time would, of course, have been the scriptures contained in the Old Testament. Then there was also the obvious matter of their lack of faith. And that lack of faith had two elements to it. Firstly, their lack of faith in the written Word of God (if you don't know it, how can you even begin to believe it). And their lack of faith concerning Jesus' promise that he would be resurrected.

Am I painting an accurate picture here? Well, let's look at Jesus' response to what his disciple Cleopas had said to him. Jesus' response was hardly sympathetic or even particularly kind for that matter.

In fact, he immediately reprimanded both disciples. After all, they had both been involved in conversing and reasoning - conversing and reasoning, which had drawn pretty negative conclusions. Once these two disciples had had their say - and painted a fairly dismal picture, it was Jesus' time to pitch in. To paraphrase what he said, it went something like this - you are behaving like fools, you are demonstrating that you neither sufficiently know what is written by the prophets, (the Old Testament scriptures), and don't have the faith to understand or believe what they say about me. This is not the first time Jesus used the term "fools" when referring to certain people. I don't believe it is meant in the same insulting way it is today.

The biblical term for fool usually refers to those who lack wisdom, knowledge, and understanding. To expand on that a little further, those who lack knowledge and understanding because they have been careless and negligent and who should know better. The term fool is not intended as an insult; it is, however, a clear rebuke. And the rebuke, in this case, was, I believe, along the lines of you really should know better. In fact, as my disciples, I *expect* you to know better. Jesus went on to say: "Aught not the Christ to have suffered these things and to enter into his glory?" To paraphrase, Jesus said: surely, you should have known that I would have to be crucified in order for me to be raised again?

What Jesus did next is really the very crux of this first chapter of Apples of Gold. For me, it profoundly exemplifies what it really means to be a disciple of Jesus. It absolutely crystallises the meaning of "walking in the spirit." And it is also the very foundation and substance of biblical wisdom, knowledge, and understanding. What is it? It is this:

Beginning at Moses and all the Prophets, he expounded to them, in all the scriptures, the things concerning himself.

Before going further, I want to make a couple of observations, which I believe are of considerable significance and could be of great benefit to the Christian today. The first observation is this: Having listened to Cleopas, Jesus didn't even begin to continue the conversation. I mean, he didn't even begin to continue the conversation - at the level that Cleopas and his fellow-disciple had been talking. He totally dismissed it but immediately took the conversation up to a completely higher level. The word of God level.

There is an unmissable lesson here for today's believers. There is an unmissable lesson here for today's church. The lesson is: God does not and will not operate at our level. He will not be party to our reasonings debates and deliberations. Particularly when they are devoid of a sound knowledge of scripture. No, He functions at the Word level. And so must we. He did then, and he still does now. Yes, Jesus drew alongside Cleopas and the other disciple, yes, he drew alongside to hear their conversation, but with the sole purpose of changing it, and changing it without further deliberations. Changing it abruptly. Changing it without giving them a choice in the matter. Changing it without explanation and changing it without their consent or agreement.

Firstly, he reprimanded them because their reasoning and conversation were not sufficiently "word" based. Then he began to quite literally flood them with the word of God. In other words, he began to urgently compensate for their ignorance and lack of understanding. The distance from Jerusalem to Emmaus is about seven miles. That is approximately a three-hour walk. If we assume that Jesus joined them at an early stage of their journey, that indicates that these two disciples, though they began by doing all the talking, ultimately said very little, and Jesus said a great deal.

Much of their journey was spent, quite literally "in the word" as we Christians call it these days. Now that is something worth noting.

How much of our journey is spent *talking about* church, kingdom, and events in our Christian lives? How much time, by comparison, do we spend, personally reading, studying, learning, and listening to what the Word of God has to say to each one of us as we walk out our own journey? How much of our church conversation is scripturally based, inspired, and informed?

The road from Jerusalem to Emmaus can serve as a kind of analogy of our own lives. An analogy of our own journey and spiritual walk. Only, instead of it being a mere seven miles in distance, and around three hours in time, the miles can represent the distance through life we have traveled so far. It strikes me that if Jesus had not intervened in the lives of these two disciples, as they journeyed, their conversation, perception, and outlook would have been exactly the same halfway through their journey, say at the three and a half mile stage, as it had been when they initially set out.

To further emphasise my point, I believe it would have also been the same three quarters way through their journey, say at roughly the five mile stage. It would still have been the same only by this time it would have become quite repetitive and monotonous. Then, towards the end of their journey, their same conversation might be leaning towards being fairly tedious and quite frankly - boring. You see, until Jesus joined them during their journey, the only frame of reference they had was their own. Their own experience of the events that had taken place around them. Their own understanding of those events. And their own interpretation of those events.

Furthermore, by their conversation and their reasonings, they were inadvertently, gradually and incrementally, affirming and reinforcing each other's views. Views that were not firmly scripturally based and which were fundamentally flawed.

Instead of their views being formed by the Lord, they should be seeking - they were being formed by the company they were keeping.

Imagine if Cleopas and the other disciple were to journey not seven miles but seventy. Imagine had they lived today with our modern technology, and journeyed seven hundred miles. How about seven thousand miles. And all the time being limited by their own understanding of those events. I think that regardless of the length of their journey, their understanding, their conversation, and their deliberations would remain the same. The same regardless of distance. The same regardless of time. Whether the journey lasted three hours, three years, thirty years, or more, they would have the same flawed understanding. The same deliberations. The same conversation. In a fairly short space of time, they would have nothing new to say. Conversation, at least concerning their knowledge and understanding of God, would have inevitably become dull, extremely repetitive, lacklustre, and uninspiring - to say the least.

Is all this of relevance today? Is it of relevance to your life and mine as Christians, as disciples of Jesus? The very same Jesus who walked and talked with Cleopas on the Emmaus Road. Is it of relevance to today's Church? I certainly think it is. What do you think? Where are you on your journey? Where am I on mine? Where are we each on our spiritual walk? What is the nature of our spiritual conversation? What have *we* got to say about the things of God?

However, Cleopas and his companion were not destined to become repetitive, dull, lacklustre, and uninspiring disciples. Why? Simple; because the newly risen Christ came alongside them as they walked, interrupted their conversation, challenged their thinking and dramatically and radically changed their conversation. How? By immediately impacting them with the "revelation" word of God.

To quite shamelessly exploit the conceptual framework of this book, let me say this: Using the vast palette of The Artist's inspired and eternal Word, Jesus lavishly and masterfully coloured in technicolour and multi-dimensional imagery, their monochrome, one-dimensional world! Is my language too colourful, too flamboyant? Perhaps, but consider this:

Beginning at Moses,

*And **all** the Prophets,*

He expounded to them,

*In **all** the scriptures,*

The things concerning himself.

There are thirty-nine books in the Old Testament. Over an approximate three-hour period, Jesus taught these two disciples, from each and every one of those books - *every scripture* - that related to him. Just for biblical clarity and accuracy: It says, "Beginning at Moses." The first mention of Moses is the account of his birth in Exodus. Moses is attributed as having written the first five books of the bible. Beginning at Moses would include the book of Genesis. Also, fifteen of the Old Testament books are by authors, specifically called prophets. Figures such as Noah, Abraham, Samuel, King David are also referred to as prophets, albeit in a slightly different sense. Additionally, the above verse states that Jesus expounded to them in (or from) *all* the prophets and *all* the scriptures.

My personal understanding is that the above verse indicates that Jesus revealed to those two disciples, scriptures from all thirty-nine books of the Old Testament that refer to him. I personally find that to be remarkable, amazing, wonderful, breathtaking, astonishing, exhilarating, incredibly exciting - and personally very empowering. The plain fact is - it is only Jesus -The Lord Jesus Christ, who can truly, both reveal - and interpret the scriptures to us. You will remember from the gospels that whilst Jesus spoke to the multitudes in parables - he always then took his disciples aside privately to explain the meaning of the parables. But it was only his disciples who had that privilege.

Furthermore, as would be later written in the gospels, Jesus told his disciples that after he had ascended to the Father that he would send another Comforter who, he said, is the Holy Spirit and that he:

- Was the Spirit of truth

- Would come in his (Jesus') name

- Would lead them into all truth

- Would teach them all things

- Would speak what the Father in heaven spoke

- Would speak of what he saw (in the heavenly realm - things pertaining to God's kingdom)

- Would show them things to come

He also promised - I will not leave you comfortless (without help, direction, and instruction). I will come to you. I will never leave or forsake you. I will always be with you. *(Bible Ref: John 14:16-18 & v 26 / John 16:13-15)*

There was a window in time in the lives of those two disciples. A window in time, which changed their lives forever. It was to completely change their outlook for the rest of their lives. It was to dramatically and radically change their understanding of God's Kingdom on earth. And it would change their understanding of 'church' and how it was truly designed to function.

And it would particularly reinforce to them what it truly means to be a disciple of Jesus Christ.

And that window was their encounter with Jesus on the Emmaus Road. An encounter that broke them open dispelled and discarded their ill-informed misconceptions and misunderstanding and flooded them with the revelation word of God.

What do I mean by the "revelation" word of God? I mean this: That the meaning and the spiritual interpretation of the scriptures, *all* the scriptures, was personally and intimately revealed to them by Jesus himself. *That* is precisely what happened on the Emmaus Road. *That* is the picture that is presented. I just don't think it could be any clearer; I truly don't.

Here we see two of Jesus' early disciples walking down a road, essentially talking about kingdom events as they were occurring at their time. Their time being the days and the culture in which they lived and the events taking place around them. Just like two Christians walking together down a road today in the 21st Century and talking about church, God's kingdom, and what's happening in the church. What's going on in the churches in their area and perhaps discussing what they are hoping God will do, or that they are praying for breakthrough and so on. That is, of course, all good, but I'm sure that like me, you find there to be quite an array of views and opinions. Some may say we need God to send revival. Others perhaps that we need more unity. Or that we need to pray more, or that we need to be more holy.

There are differing views on types of church, types of service, styles of leadership, expressions of worship, styles of worship, methods of outreach and evangelism, and so on. That is all perfectly understandable, perfectly alright, and perfectly good and normal. But like the two disciples on the Emmaus Road, how much of our conversations, deliberations, and reasonings - as we seek to walk-out our spiritual life and service, is perhaps wrongly shaped and informed by our own limited perceptions and lack of understanding? Should we maybe honestly ask ourselves just how long we've been having these conversations? Have *our* conversations, reasonings, and deliberations become circuitous and repetitive, even to the extent that they have become ingrained in our spiritual culture, terminology, language, and thinking? And perhaps, like those two early disciples, are we possibly misinterpreting and misunderstanding events? And possibly, just like them, not really seeing things in the light of scripture - to the extent, as disciples, that we should?

Remember, these two men already knew Jesus, in the same way, if you are a Christian today, that you and I know him. They had been exposed to his teaching for a number of years. But they were still clearly lacking something. I believe that is why Jesus joined them on their walk. I want to say something at this point, something of great importance, and it's this: They didn't invite Jesus to join them, to accompany them - they didn't have to. Why? Simple: because they already belonged to him. They were *his* disciples, his friends, people he had already called and chosen. Just like you and me. What's my point? It's this: As Christians, we don't have to invite Jesus to walk with us - he already does.

The picture here is that he came alongside them, the bible says he drew near. And that he did so - to specifically to impart the word of God to them.

To impart the word of God precisely for the stage of the journey they were on and the distance they had already travelled. And that "word" was to fill the void in their understanding - at the very point of their need. They were confused. They were bewildered. They were discouraged. And they were despondent. More specifically, what had happened on their spiritual walk, their walk with Jesus over the past few years, now just didn't make sense to them.

The solution to their dilemma. The remedy for their discouragement. The cure for their confusion. The antidote to their misunderstanding was this: Not more talk - but:

- To hear from Jesus

- Directly and personally - from Jesus

- The resurrected Jesus

But, specifically - to receive the scriptures - *from him*. Scriptures which related to their personal circumstances. As was the case for them then, I believe the very same applies to us now.

So what is there for us to learn here? Just like those two early disciples on the Emmaus Road, many of you reading this book already have a history with Jesus. You know him, and you know you were called by him. You may have been on your Christian journey for a few years or for many years. You are aware of world events and the current societal factors that affect all of us. You are also conscious of matters concerning your own church life. You have your own opinions of where the church is in your area, nationally and even wider. And it is only right and normal that, just like the two disciples on the Emmaus Road, you talk about, discuss, and perhaps even deliberate these matters with other believers. After all, we love the Lord; we love one another; we pray for the church to be strong, effective, and successful. We also long to see God move, to see the nations impacted, and to see many people saved. We must, after all, as Jesus himself said - be about our father's business. But - and this, I believe, is the very crux of the matter, the very point of this episode in the biblical narrative and the crystal clear message that this particular picture' seeks to convey:

Just how much of our thinking, our understanding, our interpretation of events, and our subsequent conversations and deliberations, are influenced and informed by the now - revelation word of God?

- What does God have to say about your situation?
- What does God have to say about your church?
- What does God have to say about the churches in your area?
- What does God have to say about your place and your responsibilities in the church?
- What does God have to say about the events in your nation?
- What does God have to say about where you and I are on our journey?
- What is God saying to us now, today, about our own spiritual walk?

Just like those two early disciples - are we aware that Jesus himself - the very same resurrected Christ, is walking beside us. He is seeking to draw near. But what for?

- To make us feel better?
- To make us happy?
- To make our lives problem and trouble-free?
- To just tell us everything is going to be OK?

No - He seeks to draw near - to accompany us on our walk. First and foremost - to impart to each and every one of us, each and every one of his disciples - the revelation word of God.

Is it possible for us, as Christians, to go through this life without understanding the will of God?

Is it possible for us, as we journey on our own Emmaus Road, to be confused and uncertain about the church and about kingdom?

Is it possible for us to not know where we are going or what we are supposed to be doing?

Is it possible for us to then be stuck in a cycle of religious routines, endless reasonings, and deliberations and the same old Christian/church, cliches, and rhetoric?

I believe it is. Why? Because when we fail to allow Jesus to personally speak the word of God into our lives, to expound the word of God to us, to impart his word to us at the point of our need and according to the stage of our journey - and throughout our journey - the outcome is inevitable.

At the risk of over-spiritualising things, but I feel it's a risk worth taking, I want to say this:

Those two disciples didn't recognise the revelation word of God walking beside them. Many Christians today are the same.

A Sunday Sermon, a midweek bible study and a ten minute 'quiet time' in the word each day - does not and cannot equate to *walking with* the personal and direct revelation word of God. There is a world of difference between hearing sermons and bible teaching from the pulpit and hearing and receiving personally, specifically and directly, from Jesus himself.

Many Christians today are familiar with the message of the bible - but not with its meaning as it specifically applies to them. For the three years before his death and resurrection, Jesus taught by sermons and parables. Following his resurrection, he walked and talked personally and intimately alongside his disciples, imparting and expounding the scriptures to them.

Many Christians today are aware of and even familiar with Jesus, the teacher, before his death on the cross. But they are not familiar with Jesus the "living word of God" following his resurrection.

To affirm my point, we shall learn later that it was *after* those two early disciples received the revelation word of God that their "eyes were opened" so that they then recognised Jesus.

Previously, they knew him only as a teacher. But now they knew him as the resurrected, living word

of God. Moving on now as they approach Emmaus, following what was, in essence, a three hour time of fellowship with the Lord, during which time he expounded the scriptures to them. The bible says that when the two disciples had reached where they wanted to go, Jesus seemed intent on travelling further. They persuaded him to spend the night with them because it was now evening and getting late. The next thing we learn is that they sat down together for a meal. Five distinct things then occurred, which are truly astonishing, remarkable, wonderful, and extremely relevant and significant for us today.

- He broke bread and gave it to them.

- Their eyes were immediately opened, and they suddenly knew (recognised) who he was.

- He then vanished out of their sight. He quite literally disappeared.

- They talked about how their hearts had burned within them whilst Jesus had walked with them and opened the scriptures to them.

- They then set off to return to Jerusalem even though it had been their initial intention to stay in Emmaus.

He broke bread and gave it to them.

The breaking of bread has huge significance for the Christian. It symbolises the Passover, the atoning blood of Christ's sacrifice, and his body, which was broken for us. And the breaking of bread, in remembrance of those things, is something we are commanded to do regularly and reverently. What happened here at Emmaus is clearly representative of that. It resonates with events at Jesus' last supper with his twelve disciples before his crucifixion only days earlier. What we also refer to as communion is representative of the new covenant we have with God through Christ. This covenant also represents a bond, a union, a partnership, a friendship, and a relationship.

The sub-heading of this chapter is - The Road to Revelation and Relationship. On the road from Jerusalem to Emmaus, Jesus drew near to these two disciples to remind them - and demonstrate to them that to be his disciple, they must always be attuned to his word - quite literally, every step of the way. We generally consider the day of Pentecost to be the birth of the church. This event, the Emmaus Road event, was, in fact, the very first day of a new era, a new dispensation, the dispensation of the Resurrected Jesus. The Resurrected Jesus was walking alongside his disciples.

As it was then - is precisely the same today. And on that very first day of the New Testament church - literally the dawn of a new era. A new age. The church age. Jesus was dramatically demonstrating from the onset of the new church age, on the very first day in fact, that it is fundamentally crucial that his church - then and now, must walk out their lives - intimately in step with him. And specifically, in-step with his voice. The voice of the living word of God. The Revelation Word of God - revealed to us - to each one of us - *by him*. Otherwise, like those two early disciples, we may find that our walk becomes one of disillusionment, dismay, discouragement, disappointment, and even confusion. Like them, it will be reflected in our conversation - or indeed the lack of it, about God, his church, and his kingdom. For me, the breaking of bread, in this context, is also significant in two other ways.

Firstly, Jesus had just spent time breaking open the scriptures to those disciples. And the scriptures, as we know, is the bread of life. Jesus had, in effect, dramatically demonstrated, even acted out, on the Emmaus Road journey, the edict from God from ages past - that "man cannot live by bread alone but by every word that proceeds from the mouth of God." Jesus breaking bread with these two disciples was a confirmation and a culmination of the fact that he had just spent three hours breaking the bread of life open to them. I feel that I simply cannot stress enough that these things were done then - at the very birth of the church - for us to take note of - now!

Secondly, upon reaching Emmaus, Jesus and those two disciples didn't sit down to break bread in the sense that we regard it today, i.e., the act of sharing communion. They had sat down at the end of a long and tiring day to eat a meal together. That is what friends and families do. So, the breaking of bread in this context is also about friendship and relationship. These disciples had just experienced the power and the benefit of the revealed word of God on their journey from Jerusalem to Emmaus. In essence, now they were being reminded of the fact that they were in a relationship with Jesus. They were quite simply breaking the bread of friendship—a friendship which affirmed and consolidated their relationship.

In order for a Christian, any Christian, to truly experience receiving the revelation word of God, they simply MUST be prepared to spend real time in prayer. And real-time reading the bible. And that needs to be a real and regular part of their life. Yes, that takes discipline. And like any form of discipline, it requires a degree of sacrifice. It is fundamentally core to being a disciple of Christ that a Christian is prepared to discipline themselves to truly follow him. The three hours of personal teaching from the scriptures followed by intimate time spent together, as represented in this narrative, is symbolic of such a life. That is precisely what it represents:

Their eyes were opened.

As a result of Jesus breaking some bread at their meal and giving it to them, these two disciples eyes were suddenly opened, and they recognised who he was. That he was, in fact, the Jesus they had known before his crucifixion, and it seems, they had still thought was dead until that very moment. You will recall from the beginning of this chapter that when Jesus joined them on their walk, their eyes were prevented from seeing him. And only now were their eyes opened. Clearly, this was spiritual blindness, spiritual blindness which was only cured by exposure, firstly to the revelation word of God, i.e., imparted to them by Jesus himself.

Then when their relationship was restored through sharing a meal and the breaking of bread. Hence - *revelation and relationship*. We cannot fail to notice that even during the three-hour journey when Jesus was expounding the scriptures to them, they still hadn't known who he was. It was only when they broke bread together that their spiritual eyes were opened. That is simply remarkable. Again, this serves to emphasise and reinforce the relationship aspect of our walk with God. Putting it plainly, intimacy, and relationships of any kind require quality time spent together.

No relationship can either be formed, nurtured, or sustained by an investment of a mere ten minutes a day. Neither can mere attendance at church meetings realistically be considered to constitute a real relationship with God. Like any other relationship - you get out what you put in. I believe this event also teaches us clearly that a Christian life based on the word alone is insufficient. Firstly, without an actual relationship with Jesus, how can he expound, explain, or break open the scriptures to us? This helps explain certain types of Christians who seem to know lots of scriptures but are legalistic, formal, hard, and rigid. That was, in fact, Jesus' criticism of the Pharisees. They were all 'word' but no relationship. That also is precisely why they got so much wrong. And that is precisely why they didn't recognise Jesus for who he was.

Consider here our two disciples on the Emmaus Road. Blind to Jesus at the start of their journey, but spiritual eyes wide open at the end of it. Equally is the situation where some Christians are all 'relationship' but little or no word. The concern in such cases is that ultimately, they will rely on their feelings, not spiritual word informed facts. That was the initial state of those two disciples. Yes, they knew Jesus and had done for some time. But when things appeared to have gone wrong, or not worked out as they thought or 'felt' they should, all they had to rely on was - their feelings. And they proved to be wrong. Just what kind of relationship would it be if a man just 'talked at' his wife but spent little or no time with her? Equally, what kind of relationship would it be if he did spend time with her but never spoke to her? A real relationship - a healthy and functioning relationship, requires a balance of both.

He vanished out of their sight.

Once Jesus had accomplished what he set out to do with these two disciples, now that their spiritual eyes had been opened to these things, now that they were back on the right 'road,' he simply vanished. But the bible says specifically that he vanished "out of their sight." That in itself is significant. If we, as Christians, are going to learn from this amazing Emmaus Road event, then we might as well learn as much as we can. So, he vanished out of their sight. So much of this event deals with the issue of sight - spiritual sight.

Firstly, at the start of their journey (and remember, we are all on a journey), he was physically there, but they couldn't see it was him. That is, they didn't know who he was.

Secondly, having then received the revelation word, (lots of it) spent time with Jesus, both on the road and over a meal, and then breaking bread with him, their spiritual eyes were opened, and they could see him. So now they did know who he was.

Finally, now that they could see him and knew it was Jesus - he vanished out of their sight.

What am I saying? I'm saying this; he only vanished "out of their sight." He was still there, but now they just couldn't see him.

But, because the essential elements of what it takes to be a disciple had been re-established and restored, there was simply no need for them to see him.

Again, as it was then, so it is now. As it was with them, so it is with us. A disciple of Jesus is a disciple of Jesus. Whether it was two thousand years ago or today in the 21st century. Nothing has changed.

The bible says that we walk by faith and not by sight. That the just shall live by faith. Faith, after all, is quite simply believing something that we cannot see. But once we have heard the revelation word of God, it becomes so real to us that we don't need to see him in order to believe. Jesus said, my sheep (my disciples) hear my voice. Jesus promised that he would always be with us and that he would never leave or forsake us.

<u>They talked about how their hearts had burned within them.</u>
Here we see a dramatic shift in the conversation between these two disciples—a complete turnaround. Remember how negative and downcast they were at the start of their journey. Negative and downcast due to wrong perceptions. Wrong perceptions due to wrong thinking. Wrong thinking due to poor general knowledge

of the scriptures. And wrong thinking due to an absence of the revelation 'now' word of God. But now they were talking with passion, with excitement, with hope, and with a newly fired-up enthusiasm. Why? Because they had been filled with the word of God! Consequently, their understanding, their perceptions, and their thinking were now coloured, framed, and seen through the lens of scripture.

There are two crucial elements to being a disciple of Jesus. Firstly, we must firmly establish within our understanding that to be a disciple of Jesus - we simply *must* be disciples of his word. How can a person truly say they are following a leader but not know what that leader stands for, what they teach, and what they have to say? Secondly, as disciples, we must aspire to develop a good understanding of the written word, the scriptures. Remember, the first thing Jesus did when he joined these two disciples as they walked was to reprimand them concerning that very thing.

We must also follow his spoken word. By that, I mean the things he says to us by his Spirit. That is what I mean by the revelation - now - word of God. That is precisely what Jesus did all through their three-hour journey - he *spoke* to them. Yes, he spoke to them from the scriptures, but he didn't simply quote historical verses of scripture. No, he expounded the scriptures to them. He opened them up and personally and intimately explained the scriptures to them. He brought them to life. He made them current and relevant to the times those two disciples were living in. More so, he made them relevant to the lives and circumstances of those two disciples at that time. He made the scriptures relevant to the very stage of the journey they were on. Not just the physical journey from Jerusalem to Emmaus but the journey of their understanding, the journey of their spiritual walk, and their personal journey in the word of God. I believe that during those three intense word-packed hours, Jesus brought them up to date, up to speed. He raised their game.

He took them to the level of understanding that disciples of his should be.

He specifically expounded to them, beginning at Moses and all the Prophets - the things concerning himself. Therefore, on that three-hour walk, they continually learned more and more - about Jesus. They continually understood more and more - about Jesus. Throughout their journey, Jesus continued to reveal *himself* to them. And he did so - up close, intimately and personally. That was one-on-one personal revelation. That was one-on-one personal teaching. And that was a one-on-one personal relationship. When Jesus then disappeared out of their sight, do you think he then lost the ability to speak to them? Do you think they then lost the capacity to hear his voice? I certainly don't think so.

The term "out of sight - out of mind" may well apply to some situations, to some relationships, but not to this one. Yes, still today, Jesus, who is out of our sight, out of sight to us his 21st Century disciples, nevertheless is still present and still able to speak to us.

But, you may say, that was there, that was then, and that was them. What about us, what about here and what about now? Well, has Jesus changed? Is a disciple of Jesus different now to a disciple then? Does Jesus do things differently now? Because the obvious answer to all these questions is, of course - No. Christians today should take great encouragement from the lessons learned from the Emmaus Road journey.

Then they set off to return to Jerusalem.

Now this is indeed, fascinating. On the road from Jerusalem to Emmaus Jesus changed their thinking. Their changed thinking vastly improved their understanding and their outlook. Now their improved understanding and outlook was about to change their direction. It was going to completely reverse their original direction. You will recall that as they had been approaching Emmaus, the two disciples had encouraged Jesus to spend the night with them because it was evening. Their intention had been to stay in Emmaus that night, and perhaps longer. Perhaps they were residents of Emmaus and, disappointed at what had happened in Jerusalem, they, like one of their fellow disciples, Peter, who proclaimed "I go fishing," were giving up their lives as disciples and going home and back to their old lives. How many believers today, similarly, and tragically walk away from following Jesus, through a lack of understanding?

If only they had waited a little longer. If only they had listened a little more. No sooner had Jesus vanished from their sight; these two disciples turned on their heels and went back to where they had just come from. They went back to where they had been running from. They went back into the fellowship of the other disciples. They went back to 'church." They went back to where they truly belonged. They were back in the fold. They were back in the game. You see, wrong thinking had them going on the wrong road and going in the wrong direction. Until Jesus drew near. Yes, he drew near even when they were on the wrong road and going in the wrong direction. He does that!

He did it then, and he still does it today.

Let's enjoy the journey!

Thomas Malone

Chapter Two

The Wedding at Cana

(*Pouring out your blessing*)

Gospel of John Chapter 2 verses 1-11

On the third day there was a wedding in Cana of Galilee, and the mother of Jesus was there. ²Now both Jesus and His disciples were invited to the wedding. ³And when they ran out of wine, the mother of Jesus said to Him, "They have no wine."

⁴Jesus said to her, "Woman, what does your concern have to do with Me? My hour has not yet come." ⁵His mother said to the servants, "Whatever He says to you, do it." ⁶Now there were set there six waterpots of stone, according to the manner of purification of the Jews, containing twenty or thirty gallons apiece.

⁷Jesus said to them, "Fill the waterpots with water." And they filled them up to the brim. ⁸And He said to them, "Draw some out now, and take it to the master of the feast." And they took it. ⁹When the master of the feast had tasted the water that was made wine, and did not know where it came from (but the servants who had drawn the water knew), the master of the feast called the bridegroom. ¹⁰And he said to him, "Every man at the beginning sets out the good wine, and when the guests have well drunk, then the inferior. You have kept the good wine until now!"

¹¹This beginning of signs Jesus did in Cana of Galilee, and manifested His glory; and His disciples believed in Him.

This is the story where Jesus turns water into wine. There are a number of factors in this event that particularly stand out to me.

Firstly, this was the first-ever recorded miracle performed by Jesus. I think it's highly significant that Jesus should choose a wedding celebration as the setting for the launch of his ministry, which included the performance of his first recorded miracle. This was a proper family wedding. So, clearly, he had family ties with the bride and groom. Some of his disciples were also there, but more significantly, so was his mother. Why do I think the wedding venue is significant?

Because a wedding celebrates the coming together of man and woman who have been drawn together by the wonderful power of love. Love of such uniqueness, attraction, and strength that they want only one another for their entire lives. A love so strong that they are convinced that the object of their desire and attraction, a desire and attraction that excludes all others, is all they each need to fulfill them for the rest of their lives.

That alone clearly is the substance at the very heart and core of the message of the Bible, the work of the Holy Spirit, and the focus of the gospel. A man before he meets the one who is to become the love of his life, the one he somehow meets or is introduced to during the course of his everyday existence, is a man alone and incomplete. Equally, a woman may have everything life has to offer, but at the very core of her being is a desire to meet that one, that significant other. There is within all of us that in-built emotional and psychological need for personal and intimate love.

So it is with God. We are all, at a deeper level than emotional and psychological need, spiritually alone, and incomplete. And though we may not know what that need is, we still feel it and go through life, for the most part, knowing something is missing.

Yes, we may have parents, family, friends, and we may indeed have a husband or wife. We still all have that intrinsic need within us for a deeper and more personal intimacy. In that respect, we are alone in the sense that we are in this world, but we don't really understand it. Whenever we stop and think about it, we don't know who we are, where we came from as human beings (unless you have chosen to be duped by the ludicrous Darwinian 'monkey' theory). What is life really all about? Where we are headed in life, and what good or ill lies before us? Or indeed or what happens when we die?

The clear and wonderful message of the gospel is that God wants a relationship with us, with each and every one of us. A unique, intimate and personal relationship. A lifetime relationship. A lifelong relationship. And even more - an eternal relationship. As a man without a woman is incomplete in the physical and emotional sense, so a man or woman without a relationship with God is also incomplete but in a greater, deeper, wider and higher sense. If, through a love relationship with a partner, a person becomes emotionally and psychologically complete, so only through a love relationship with God, can a person become spiritually complete.

The bible tells us, that our relationship with God is broken because of sin. But that the relationship can be restored and renewed. Our renewed relationship with God, like the love relationship between a man and a woman, can only occur when there is a meeting. An introduction between both parties. A meeting that leads to and which culminates in the joining of them both together in a permanent binding commitment to one another. Just like a marriage.

Let me quickly justify and ratify that statement. Marriage is a legal contract. A contract that binds two people together under terms upon which they are willing to enter into and upon which they both agree. The comparison is this: the New Testament of the bible could also be termed, the New Agreement, or New Contract.

The New Testament contract sets out the terms presented by God whereby people can agree to accept the terms established by God, in order to enter into a relationship with him, through his son Jesus.

That is the reason I feel Jesus chose a wedding celebration as the setting for the launch of his ministry and his first public miracle. The wedding at Cana symbolises the fact that Jesus came to restore us (the bride) to himself (the groom) and, in so doing, making us whole, through our love relationship with him. And, in so doing, restoring us into a full relationship with God.

The second element to this story that impacts me concerns what I call - personal obedience to the revelation word of God.

In verse five, even before Jesus told the servants what to do, his mother makes what is to my mind one of the most potent statements in all scripture (and that's saying something.) She said, "Whatever he says to you, do it." It's as if she knew (and she surely did know) that what he was going to tell them to do in response to the presenting situation would be unusual, different, unconventional, impractical, illogical, or even perhaps, unintelligible. Which it was - naturally speaking that is. Remember this was Jesus' very first public miracle. Surely he was establishing a precedent. He was making a point. Or to put it another way, he was starting out as he intended to continue.

In response to being told that the wedding party had no wine or perhaps had run out of wine, depending on how you interpret the passage, Jesus' response was to tell those serving at the wedding to fill six large empty stone waterpots, with water.

Well, just what sense does that make? It was the wine they needed, not water. The servants at the wedding did as Jesus instructed them. It is worthy of note that it doesn't just say they filled the jars, but that they filled them to the brim. In other words, they were so filled that you couldn't possibly get any more water in the jars. The jars were spilling over.

The next instruction from Jesus was that they should then pour the water out for the governor of the feast to try. Can you imagine the anxiety and trepidation felt by those servants? Why? Because people were expecting wine, but the servants had just personally filled the jars with water. Now they were being told to pour out this water - to people who were expecting wine. But in pure and simple obedience to the words spoken by Jesus, they followed his instructions.

Surely herein is a clear lesson and a key kingdom principle for the Christian today who truly desires to be obedient to God and to see him powerfully operate both in and through their lives. What is it? It's this; supernatural outcomes are seldom achieved by natural means. Supernatural outcomes result from acts of faith and obedience. Faith and obedience in the face of what we may not understand. Faith and obedience, even though what we feel prompted to do, might not make sense to us. Faith and obedience that may well find us operating outwith the norm of current trends or the culture surrounding us, both religious and secular. Faith and obedience to the voice of God and to the revelation word of God.

Too often, believers expect supernatural outcomes but fail to exercise any faith or obedience, which is an essential part of the process. Often when we feel led or prompted by the Lord, it challenges our thinking, our logic, and our experience thus far. If we are only willing to do or say the normal, the natural, the understandable, and the predictable, then we simply don't need God's involvement. We can do those things all by ourselves. If we expect supernatural outcomes, we must be prepared and willing, just like the servants at the wedding at Cana, to take supernatural action. Yes, that may, at times, cause us to feel anxious, vulnerable, exposed, or fearful of failure, embarrassment, or even ridicule. That, as I understand it, is precisely the life of faith and walking in the spirit. An ordinary life can only expect limited and ordinary outcomes. Living a spiritual life; one of faith and obedience has no limitations.

What happened next was a miracle. Furthermore, it was the first recorded miracle that Jesus ever performed. Raising a man from the dead was not the first miracle he chose to perform. Neither was it healing a leper, restoring the legs of a lame man, or giving sight to a blind man. His first miracle was to turn mere water into the finest of wine. I think that this speaks volumes and that it should particularly speak volumes to the church. Jesus came to earth from heaven to restore and usher in the kingdom of God and to build his church. Yet he embarked upon this universally significant and eternally important task - by turning water into wine.

Surely a more pressing need would have been more appropriate, one that demonstrated the compassion of God or the seriousness of sin. Say the healing of the sick or the dramatic conversion of a sinner. Yet it was this that he chose to do.

When the jars of water were served to the crowd, it had become wine. The convener of the wedding commented that it was not just good wine, but he said it was the best wine.

Verse eleven says: "This was the beginning of miracles that Jesus did in Cana of Galilee, which manifested his glory, and his disciples believed on him."

The bible clearly states here that turning water into wine glorified God. It also states that it greatly impacted his disciples and increased their faith.

Thirdly, the wedding at Cana and the miracle of water being turned into wine speaks to me of the function of the church. Jesus, without question, was the most important guest at that wedding in Cana. As the Head of the Church, Jesus is, of course, the most important person in the church today. When the wine had run out at the wedding in Cana, Jesus simply made more. He *wanted* the blessing to be poured out. He wanted joy to be poured out. He wanted the celebration to be poured out. He wanted the intoxication of happiness, friendship, and fellowship to be poured out.

So he created more wine. In today's church, Jesus is present at every gathering, and he still wants such blessing to be poured out. He doesn't want his church to be a dry and tedious experience - like a wedding celebration that has no wine.

At Cana, the wine was the substance, the fruit of the vine, that made the party flow. In the church today it is the Holy Spirit (also the fruit of the Vine) that makes the church rejoice and celebrate in praise, worship, and fellowship. At Cana it was Jesus who commanded, directed and created the wine that was to then be poured out.

In the church, wherever it gathers today, it is still Jesus who releases the pouring out of His Spirit, which is what the wine is symbolic of. I think it's hugely important, significant, and relevant that we should take note of what Jesus did at Cana in order to meet what were natural needs. Why? Because it is still how he operates in the church today to meet spiritual needs - If we let him!

Firstly, he told the servants at the wedding to fill empty waterpots with water. We have already noted that his mother told the servants to do whatever Jesus told them to do. What I see here is that the empty clay vessels represent the individual Christian today. The bible refers to God's people as being clay in his hands. It also says, "We have this treasure (the indwelling spirit) in earthen vessels."

The water being poured into the empty vessels represents the Holy Spirit, which is initially poured into a person at the time of conversion upon them accepting Jesus as Lord and Saviour—thereby making them able to become a Christian and have fellowship with God the Father.

It is only when that water is poured out of the vessel that it was first poured into, that it is miraculously transformed into wine. Wine that refreshes invigorates and intoxicates others with joy, happiness and celebration.

As long as the water remains in the jar it benefits only the jar. Yet the whole purpose of Jesus having the jars filled was for their contents to then be poured out to meet the needs of others. Equally today in his church, the purpose of God filling people with his life, the Holy Spirit, is that they should then pour out that life for the benefit of those around them.

Without the filling of the water pots and the pouring out of their contents at the wedding at Cana the gathering would have become a dry, possibly dull and even disappointing occasion. Many church gatherings today without the refreshing outpouring and flow of the Holy Spirit sadly often prove to be pretty much a similar experience.

There is something both incredibly rudimental and fundamental here that we simply cannot afford to miss. So many Christians today are seeking God for the outpouring of his spirit upon their own lives, their home fellowship, the church in general, and of course, upon our deeply troubled society. Yet, here in the very opening scene of Jesus' redemptive and miraculous ministry, we are given an open display and a profound demonstration of the very operation and outworking of that outpouring.

It is that the outpouring comes through the individual believer. Clay vessels, chosen by God through salvation in Christ, filled with his Holy Spirit, then poured out to a thirsty world around them. Poured out, not only in the church but also in whatever setting or situation in which they live. I truly believe that this was precisely what was modelled by Jesus at the wedding at Cana. And that it was specifically and intentionally done at the very onset of his ministry, in order to set a precedent for the church age, which was shortly to follow. He was, in fact, quite literally setting the scene, setting the scene for how the church was to work. And the role and function of every believer (the clay vessels) within that process.

The answer to the needs of the church today and of the whole of society is not simply that God should or might pour out his spirit in revival power from the hight of the glories of heaven in response to the prayers and petitions of the saints. The answer already lies within each and every born again spirit-filled believer. And that answer lies in the established reality of God's divine pattern and plan. And that pattern and plan is that every Christian should 'pour out' what they possess within. That they should willingly and obediently pour out of the new life God has already poured into them.

Even from Bible texts on the gifts of the spirit, we learn that the gifts are not given to benefit the person to whom they are given but to benefit others. We also learn that God has given gifts and grace to every believer and not just to some. But the purpose of this book is not to delve too deeply into specific doctrine. There are very many other books on those topics. Rather, I am trying to briefly paint a picture portraying the deeper meaning of some of the wonderful events from Jesus' life and ministry.

Some years ago, I attended an International Christian leaders conference in Southport, England.

During the time of prayer and worship before the conference, I was suddenly impacted by images in my spirit that relate to the biblical account of the wedding at Cana. I saw in my spirit, very large clay jars. They were about the size of a person. I saw a hand placed over the edge of the top of one of the jars with the thumb on the outside and the rest of the hand inside, so as to grip the jar.

I also saw that the jars were completely filled to the brim with red wine. As the hand then slightly shook the jar, the wine splashed out over the top. The hand then more vigorously shook and rocked the jar causing more wine to spill out. Then the jar was pushed over onto its side, causing all of the wine to spill out onto the ground.

I was prompted by the Spirit to speak this out to those around me as it came to me, which I did. That was all I received at that time. The following morning, I woke early at about 6 am with the word of God on me. The interpretation of the vision was given to me. The Lord then told me that the jars were his people and that the hand was his. He told me that just as at the wedding at Cana, his people today were "filled to the brim" with all the good things he had given them by way of teaching, sermons, revelation, and pastoral care. But they were keeping it contained within themselves - within their "vessels."

The result is that the church and, subsequently, society, was currently spiritually dry and thirsty because of what was being contained within the vessels of individual Christians instead of it being poured out. The Lord then showed me that he was going to firstly stir the wine in the vessels. If that didn't stir his church into action, he was going to shake the vessels. Finally, if that didn't work, he was going to tip the vessels over. By either process, he was intent on releasing the wine from the jars. I understand this to mean that God is going to shake his people both individually and corporately out of three things. Firstly, their self-interest, that is, thinking that their blessing is primarily for themselves. Secondly, the current perception that church is all about the Christian receiving more and more blessing, assurances, and spiritual experiences from church services whilst praying that God will somehow save the lost by some other sovereign means that doesn't involve them. Thirdly, from their comfort zones of safe and secure church attendance, whereby they predominantly receive each week from the platform ministries but fail to give (pour) out of their own gifts and ministries, both to the church and to the lost.

I believe that the greatest revelation and spiritual awakening that the church needs to rediscover is this; it needs to rediscover that God's mechanism for abundant overflowing and continual blessing is through each and every believer, as they let him pour out to others the miracle power he has placed *within them*. At the wedding at Cana, water was poured into vessels that were available. Christians today need to make themselves available for God to use them.

I personally think that the water remained water whilst it was kept in the jar. And that the miracle of it being turned into wine only occurred when the water was poured out. The transformation took place in the pouring out - in the giving away - in the giving to others.

I believe that therein is the miracle of the church. That the power of the effectiveness of the church is contained in the activation and the contribution of every single believer. The more believers who understand this *and do it*, the more vibrant, effective, and powerful the church, the body of Christ, will be. My understanding is that; *that is* God's pattern; that *is* God's plan. That *is* how God has designed the church to function. Why then try doing things in a different way? Jesus' mother knew this. What she was saying was; If you just do what he tells you (no matter how strange it may seem or illogical it might appear to be), it *will* work.

The believer possesses the "living water" in his/her vessel (body), and it becomes life-giving new wine that brings blessing to those around them; but only when it is poured out. The water that is contained, that is, kept in containment within the jars, sustains and refreshes only the person who possesses it. When it is poured out, as at the wedding at Cana, it refreshes those in need; thereby bringing miraculous new wine, which is the Holy Spirit, the very life of Christ, into the lives of others. In the text, it says specifically, "they filled the jars to the brim." When a person truly comes to Christ, he fills them with his Spirit. The bible says, "after you believed you were sealed with that Holy Spirit of promise." Peter declared in the book of Acts; "Repent and be baptised every one of you in the name of Jesus Christ for the remission of sins and you shall receive the gift of the Holy Spirit." In the book of Ephesians, Paul refers to "being filled with the fullness of God."

However, entire books have been written on that one subject alone. I merely offer these few scriptures for reference. *(Bible ref: Ephesians 1:13 / Acts 2:38 / Ephesians 3:19)*

Herein is a great learning opportunity for Christians who either don't know what the bible says about this. Or they simply don't understand it. Or they think it doesn't apply to them personally. Many sincere believers who are genuinely hungry for more of God or to understand the will of God, unnecessarily complicate their church lives and their spiritual walk because they have missed these fundamental principles:

- Be available - like the waterpots.
- Be prepared to be empty (of self) like the waterpots.
- Be willing to be filled by the Holy Spirit.
- Be willing and responsive to then being poured out. To quite literally pour out to others what you have received from God.

That, I believe, is why turning water into wine at the wedding at Cana was Jesus' very first miracle.

Because it represents the very blueprint for the flow of the believer's spiritual life in Christ. A life of continually receiving and continually giving out. I believe that each one of us is supposed to be a conduit of the life of Christ - the life of his Spirit.

With all the diversity and variety of the expression of the love of God within us as well as the operation of the spiritual gifts he has given us. That is how God meets the needs of others. That is how the kingdom grows. That is how God equips the church.

Yet many Christians spend much time, even a lifetime, earnestly seeking the will of God and praying for God to 'move' when in fact, the answer is right in front of us - and always has been. That answer is clearly demonstrated and revealed in the very first New Testament miracle performed by Jesus. Furthermore, we see in verses seven and eight of the text that no sooner had they filled the waterpots that Jesus instructed them to pour them out. It was like one action; "fill them up and pour them out." We see there that the waterpots were for one purpose; to be filled and poured out. Not to be filled and just sit there filled. Yet is that not often the picture of the church today?

Let's now briefly consider the magnitude and the capacity of the volumes of the six waterpots. It says they each contained twenty or thirty gallons. Taking the lowest capacity of twenty gallons, and there being eight pints in one gallon, do you realise that equates to around one thousand pints? That is roughly the equivalent of one thousand bottles of wine. Yes - one thousand bottles of wine! That is remarkable - to say the very least. So, in response to the wedding celebrations being a dry affair, Jesus produced (the potential for) one thousand bottles of wine. And not just ordinary wine, it was "the best wine." I think we can safely also state that it was absolutely unique wine. That clearly is an extravagant overabundance, which very powerfully makes a fundamental statement that this is not just about actual wine. No, it represents the limitless, overflowing, forever flowing and ever available, free gift of the Holy Spirit to anyone and everyone who calls upon the name of the Lord. And it represents the over-abundance of the limitless availability and provision of the Holy Spirit to the church.

As is so often the case, the things that Jesus said, taught and did, as recorded in the New Testament, are, in fact, a continuation of events already written about in the Old Testament. This also very clearly applies to the miracle of turning water into wine at the wedding at Cana. The bible teaches us that Jesus represents and embodies all the fullness of God the Father. During his three-year ministry on earth, he continued the work of God as recorded from Genesis to Malachi. He did things the way that the Holy Spirit has always done them. And in so doing, we clearly see some of the spiritual principles involved.

In that respect, the miracle of water into wine, whilst being absolutely unique, was yet another expression of some of the principles of how God works. Not just how God works, but more specifically, how he works with, in and through his people. Here are just two examples:

In 1 Kings, Chapter 17, God told Elijah, during a time of famine, to journey to Zarephath because he had commanded a widow woman who lived there to feed him. When Elijah got there, he didn't find a woman with an abundance of supplies. That would have made sense. But no, he found a woman who had a son who were themselves at the point of starvation. She told Elijah she barely had enough flour and oil for one last meal for her and her son, after which she was sure they would die. Elijah's reply to her was unusual. He told her to feed him first. He went on to explain to her that if she served him with the little that she had, that her own flour and oil would not run dry until the famine was over.

To put it another way, he was saying pour out what you've got to meet my needs, and you will discover that you have plenty and more leftover. So, like the water into wine at the wedding at Cana, the miracle was in the pouring out. The widow's ordinary food became miracle food. When? When she poured it out to meet the needs around her, and when she gave what she had to others.

That is precisely what being a Christian is really all about. It's about us giving to others. And that's how God operates. He wants to provide for people and enrich people and bless people. And he uses his people to do it through. It is incredibly important for the Christian to understand this.

The fact is, we serve a miracle-working God. But so many Christians are looking for miracles whilst entirely missing the point that *they* are the source of those miracles. Furthermore, so often, believers expect things to make sense. They wrongly expect they should understand what God is doing, what he is going to do, and what he may be asking or prompting them to do. But it made absolutely no sense (to the natural mind) why God should send a starving man to a starving woman. When we study that text, it specifically says in verse nine: "go to Zarephath because I have commanded a widow woman there to sustain (feed) you." God had already instructed that woman to give her meagre substance to someone else. At the wedding at Cana, Jesus instructed the servants to pour out the water. Today God still commands his people to give - pour out - what he has given each one of them. Remember, it was only water that the jars at the wedding at Cana were filled with, not wine. And it would have remained only water as long as it remained in the jars. It became (miraculous) wine only as it was poured out.

Furthermore, so long as it was being poured, it never ran out. Elijah's promise to the widow was if you pour it out it will never run out. So many believers today think they have little to give. Like the widow, they think they only have enough for themselves. They read the situation around them and perceive it is dry, and they call on God to change things, thinking (wrongly) that change will come from somewhere or someone else. However, just like the widow woman, we need to understand - *we* are the source of that change, *we* are the source of that provision. Just imagine what church would be like if every believer was giving of their talents and ministries instead of looking to others to provide it.

Furthermore, Elijah didn't just say feed me first, and you'll be OK, no, in verse fourteen we see that he said: "For this says the Lord God of Israel, the (your) barrel of flour neither the jar of oil will run out until the day that the Lord sends rain on the earth." Meaning, until the drought and famine are over. He was clearly stating - this is what God says. This is what God commands. This is how God works. This is how God does things. The principles that Jesus operated by at the wedding at Cana were exactly the same. In launching his earthly ministry at the wedding at Cana by turning water into wine, he was making a definitive statement, even an announcement to the world that the Kingdom of God had arrived, along with its principles of operation. I believe that the church is meant to continue to operate within these principles. The effective church simply cannot operate in the natural, and it was never intended to. As Christians, we need to ask ourselves when things aren't working out either personally or within our churches; Am I and are we, operating within the principles of the kingdom?

Let's consider for a moment what would have happened had the widow not listened to Elijah, or worse, she had listened but refused to act upon his counsel. Firstly, Elijah would have gone hungry. As such, the purposes of God at that time and in that situation would have at the least been held up and delayed. God would have had to move Elijah on to somewhere else and someone else. Imagine that! And the widow would have missed out on being part of the move of God in her life. She didn't know it, but her 'need' was pivotal to the purposes of God in her life and even to the region in which she lived.

Secondly, the widow and her son would have eaten their last meal, then that was it. Game over! By keeping her substance to herself, she would not only have denied someone in need, but she would also have denied herself and her son ongoing life-giving provisions. By staying in the natural, she would have completely missed out on the miracle of supernatural provision. Her immediate needs would have been met, albeit briefly and temporarily, but her spiritual needs would have dried up. She would in-effect have stopped the flow of the Spirit.

By keeping their water in their vessel, that is precisely what very many Christians do today. Instead of being a constant source of spiritual provision to others, they frequently find themselves in need.

Let's take a look at one other example from the Old Testament in 2 Kings, Chapter 4.

I think this story is absolutely amazing and thrilling. Within the context of the truths we are dealing with here, it really is quite impossible to miss the spiritual simplicity and profound significance of this event. A woman whose husband had been a prophet and who had been known to Elisha came to him, saying her husband had died and that a creditor was going to take her two sons into servitude (forced servanthood) in lieu of her deceased husband's unpaid debts. This poor woman's situation was truly desperate as she stood to lose everything. Elisha responded by asking her two questions.

The first seemed a little uncaring. He asked her how can I help you? I personally think he quite literally meant, what do you think I can do about it? In other words, he was acknowledging that it was a big problem. Even if, in the short term, Elisha could somehow have helped stop her sons being taken, she was still poor because her source of provision (her husband) was dead. What happened next was that Elisha switched from the natural to the spiritual. At the wedding at Cana, Jesus enacted spiritual principles that resulted in miraculous and abundant provision. And those principles were that if people in whom he has placed his life, pour that life out for the benefit of others, the supply and flow of his life-giving 'life' will be inexhaustible, unstoppable, and limitless.

Those principles are clearly seen in this Old Testament event. One of very many that are a foreshadow of what was yet to come, namely, the life of God in Christ, and the life of Christ in the believer and that life then being poured out by the church, which is His Body. We could say that the first question Elisha asked the woman was natural when he essentially said - "What can I do about it - I can't help you." The second question was spiritual. He asked her, "What do you have in your house." Or to put it another way - "What do *you* possess?" He was saying, I can't help you, but you can help yourself. He was saying; you have the answer within your own resources. All you have to do is to pour out. Her answer to Elisha was, I don't have anything in the house but a pot of oil. Now I'm sure you can see quite a contradiction in what she said. She said I don't have anything in my house. Surely, I don't have anything means - I have *nothing*. Now, nothing is nothing, and you can't do anything with nothing. Let's put it another way; you can't do anything if you *think* you have nothing. If a Christian, any Christian, thinks they have "nothing in their house" or to put it another way, nothing inside them of worth, of significance, or of benefit to others, they are, in fact, completely and totally wrong. And they fail to understand or to comprehend or appreciate just what and who they are in Christ.

But the woman went on to say, "I have nothing in my house…but (or except) a pot of oil". Let's say that again…except a pot of oil!

Elijah's widow at Zarephath said, "I only have a little." The woman speaking to Elisha here said, "I have nothing." In the church, when it comes to preaching, teaching, public speaking, evangelism, sharing their knowledge of the bible, leadership, testifying, leading others to Christ, and so on, many Christians today would give a similar response.

Such a response is largely based upon a misconception that they think they have to possess qualities such as being knowledgeable and accomplished or articulate and confident. Or even that they need to be specially trained, have a ministry title, or hold a particular qualification before they can do these things. In other words, like the two widows, they don't think they have enough. When in fact - *they do*!

What believers need to realise is that because they have the indwelling Holy Spirit, they already possess that "pot of oil." All they then need to do is to pour it out when the need arises and when a situation requires them to do so. Everything else will take care of itself.

The pouring out will achieve its purpose. Furthermore, such pouring out will increasingly release the believer into a life of service and ministry as their understanding develops and matures.

That's precisely what both Elijah and Elisha did with the two widows; they demonstrated to them that if they gave the "little" they had, even, *all* they had, to meet the needs of others - their own needs would be met. Furthermore, their actions - *and their obedience* would release unimaginable long-term personal resources. The point must be made here that Elijah and Elisha didn't 'teach' the widows what to do, in the hope that they might act on it later. No, they used the women's own immediate and personal crisis in a way that they had to learn there and then. To learn 'on the job.' To learn – *by doing!*

That, I believe, is also precisely what Jesus did at the wedding at Cana. There was a need. A big need. An immediate need. A need where there was no natural solution. He met that need by utilising the people around him to serve others - by pouring out!

At the wedding at Cana, Jesus' mother told him there was no wine. Jesus' instructions to the servants were to fill some available clay vessels with water. Note: there was no miracle in that. There was, however, obedience on the part of the servants. Had they not followed his instructions, there would have been no miracle. Church - are we listening?

But now here comes the miracle; he then instructed that they pour it out. The miracle and the abundance and the provision and the met need - was *all* in the 'pouring out.'

Elisha then told the woman to go around all of her neighbours, as many as she could, and borrow as many empty vessels as possible. He specifically said, "don't borrow just a few." Then, he said, when you have gathered all those empty vessels into your house - pour out into all those vessels. Let's take a minute here. Pour out exactly what into all those empty vessels? Pour out her 'pot of oil' into all those vessels. But that doesn't make any sense. How can a small pot of oil fill very many empty vessels? Surely that won't work. Surely that cannot work. It just isn't logical. But neither did what happened at the wedding at Cana make any sense. How did that work? None of these wonderful events make sense - in the natural. But we are not dealing with the natural. We are dealing with spiritual things. We are dealing with the spiritual and the natural. Spiritual in that it is the Spirit of Almighty God who is involved here, who lest we forget, made absolutely everything - out of absolutely nothing in the first place.

We are also dealing with the natural because all of these events involve people. They involved people then, and they involve people, you and me, now - today and every day. Why? Because from the book of Genesis onwards, the story is all about God - and us how God made us, what God wants for us, how he interacts with us. And how he empowers, leads, and guides us.

Just in case you haven't realised by now, all of these references concerning oil and wine and water refer to the Holy Spirit.

And if you are someone who has accepted Christ as Lord and Saviour and have experienced a new birth in Christ, then God's Holy Spirit lives within you. And one of the reasons he lives within you is so that you can share him - by pouring him out to others. Through Christ, you possess the oil and the wine and the (living) water. Namely - the Holy Spirit. The empty vessels are those around you who are not yet Christians. They have not yet accepted Jesus. They do not have the Holy Spirit. They are empty of the life of God.

So she borrowed as many empty vessels as she could and had them brought into her house. She then began to fill them by pouring her pot of oil into them. The bible doesn't say how many vessels she borrowed, and I think it doesn't matter. I think if it was ten or one hundred or more that it made no difference. I believe that as long as there were available empty vessels that the woman's pot of oil would have kept on pouring. Why? Because the oil was God's provision, not hers. It was God's miracle, not hers. She was merely the intermediary, the conduit, the means by which the oil was transferred from one vessel into other vessels. But her role was very important because she was the 'pourer.' Isn't it interesting that like Elijah's widow, she also became a source of blessing and provision to others as well as to herself.

Furthermore, it was initially because of her own desperate circumstances. From being poor, she became rich. From being weak, she became strong. From being a victim, she became a victor. From being found in hopeless circumstances, she gave hope to others. From being needy, she met the needs of others. From being empty, she became full. All because she was obedient to the instruction to pour out the little that she had.

Surely this is a key lesson for each and every believer in Christ today. Let us not look at what we don't have. Rather let us acknowledge and understand what we do have. And let us be prepared to serve others with it. Let us be prepared to pour out what we have in our vessel. And let us then see the vast difference that will make to the church, to the lives of those around us and indeed to our own lives. I believe this to be a fundamental, foundational, and core principle of how the church is designed to function. This is how the church of Jesus is meant to work. This is a major key to fruitfulness, release, abundance, and increase. This is a sound biblical principle that we simply cannot afford to underestimate or ignore.

So let's now round off this amazing story, this picture and indeed this chapter. When the woman filled all the vessels, she told one of her sons who were helping her to bring her another vessel. He told her there were no more. The bible then says that the oil stopped flowing - immediately. The oil stopped flowing from her 'pot' the very second there wasn't a vessel to pour it into. Immediately there was no available empty vessel - the flow stopped. The provision stopped. The life-source stopped. The miracle stopped. The 'blessing' stopped.

The meaning of empty vessel here is twofold:

Firstly, it relates to the individual believer being a willing vessel in the hands of God. Willing to empty themselves for the benefit of others. Willing to pour out their love, their compassion, their testimony, and their personal experience of God's amazing grace. Willing to pour out to others, both within and outwith the church, their knowledge of the word of God. Willing to pour out the particular talents and giftings which the bible clearly teaches that God has given each and every believer. Willing to pour out all of these things in service and ministry to those around them.

Secondly, empty vessels refer to those around us who don't yet know Christ.

In the story of the widow and her sons, as soon as there were no more empty vessels from her neighbours, the flow of oil stopped. More specifically - *her* flow of oil stopped. The miraculous flow of *'her pot of oil'* stopped. Some believers today seem to be always looking to hear something new from God. Some new ministry or a new prophecy. For God to 'do something.' Or for God to do something new. Always wanting more but not realising that the way to get more is to empty themselves of what they already have - what they already possess in their vessels. Often believers fail to realise that they are already 'filled to the brim.' And that there is no room for more.

This is by no means meant to be a criticism on my part. Rather it's an exhortation and encouragement to fellow Christians that we should more readily understand, appreciate and celebrate how incredibly rich we are in the things of God; In the "unsearchable riches of Christ." What we take for granted - the world is desperate to receive.

What I'm saying is this, the way to get more from God is to give away, to pour out what we already have. Thereby imparting to others and also then receiving more for ourselves. I have intentionally not peppered this book with scripture chapter and verse, but there are two wonderful verses that succinctly illustrate this particular spiritual principle. Proverbs 11:25 "The generous soul will be made rich, and he who waters will also be watered himself." Luke 6:38 "Give and it will be given unto you, good measure, pressed down, shaken together and running over will men put back into your bosom. For the same measure that you use, it will be measured back to you."

So - the Christian is an empty vessel that has been filled. We, in turn, should be passionately focussed on other empty vessels that have not yet been filled, and each play our part in pouring into them in whatever measure we can. I wish to make two distinctions here:

Firstly, as members of the body of Christ, we should each seek to pour out what we possess into our local church and our local community of believers. Thereby playing our part in equipping the church and building up the body of Christ. It is as we each pour out the new wine to one another that the church, like the wedding at Cana, is constantly refreshed and reinvigorated by the continual outpouring and flow of the Holy Spirit.

Secondly, as disciples of Jesus, we should each seek to actively obey the call to proclaim the gospel to a lost world. We all have our part to play in this. How? By reaching out to those around us; our family, friends, colleagues, and neighbours - all empty vessels in need of Christ.

Then, in reaching out, we should never underestimate what we possess within us. And just like the servants at the wedding at Cana, be prepared to believe that what we pour out will indeed be miraculous.

Chapter Three

Launching Out Into the Deep

(*Leaving the shores of mediocrity*)

Gospel of Luke. Chapter 5 verses 1-11

[1]So it was, as the multitude pressed about Him to hear the word of God, that He stood by the Lake of Gennesaret, [2]and saw two boats standing by the lake; but the fishermen had gone from them and were washing their nets. [3]Then He got into one of the boats, which was Simon's, and asked him to put out a little from the land. And He sat down and taught the multitudes from the boat.

[4]When He had stopped speaking, He said to Simon, "Launch out into the deep and let down your nets for a catch." [5]But Simon answered and said to Him, "Master, we have toiled all night and caught nothing; nevertheless, at Your word I will let down the net." [6]And when they had done this, they caught a great number of fish, and their net was breaking.

[7]So they signaled to their partners in the other boat to come and help them. And they came and filled both the boats, so that they began to sink. [8]When Simon Peter saw it, he fell down at Jesus' knees, saying, "Depart from me, for I am a sinful man, O Lord!"

[9]For he and all who were with him were astonished at the catch of fish which they had taken; [10]and so also were James and John, the sons of Zebedee, who were partners with Simon. And Jesus said to Simon,

"Do not be afraid. From now on you will catch men." [11]*So when they had brought their boats to land, they forsook all and followed Him.*

Here I see a very clear picture. A picture within a contextual frame that captures much of what the New Testament has to say. Firstly about the revelation word of God. Secondly about the authority of Jesus. And thirdly, about how they should inform the spiritual life of the believer and the function and purpose of the church. I also see the heart of God, what he wants, his plans and desires and how he partners with his people - the church, in the process of outworking the Great Commission. The great commission, of course, being, "Go you into all the world, preach the gospel and make disciples."

The picture begins by describing Jesus standing by the lake of Gennesaret, also known as the Sea of Galilee, and that he saw two boats and that the fishermen were not in the boats but were on land washing their nets. I see a sense of disapproval and disappointment on the part of Jesus in what he saw. He saw boats that were built to be on the sea in pursuit of fish. He also saw fishermen who were trained to be in the boats out at sea catching fish. However, the fishermen were not in the boats; consequently, they were not catching fish. The nets were on the shore being washed instead of hauling fish. And the boats were tied up at the shore.

Immediately after Jesus is presented with this scene (this picture), it becomes very evident that he intended to change it. Not just change it, but completely reverse it and turn it around. The first and immediate thing he did was to get into one of the boats. He then told Simon (Simon Peter) to cast out on the sea a little distance from the land. So, Jesus not only got into the boat, he told Peter to get into the boat as well. Then he told him to get the boat away from the shore, away from dry land, untethered from its moorings and out onto the water. That, after all, is where fishing boats are supposed to be. And where fishermen are meant to be; in their boats and on the water where the fish are.

There's a great deal that both the individual Christian and the wider church today can learn from this scene. The boats represent the church. It is meant to be out on the high and risky sea in pursuit of lost souls. Instead, it is sometimes more inclined to remain in the harbour tethered to the safely of the shore, feeling safe and secure in shallow water. Like the fishermen washing their nets, the believer can, at times, be preoccupied with attending church services and a variety of meetings. This can be likened to the fishermen washing their nets. Washing them but not using them. It is the nets that have become the focus of attention rather than the harvest that the nets were designed to catch. So, the picture that confronted Jesus was all wrong. Like the other 'pictures' that I present in this book, I see these scriptural passages as microcosms of church and the individual believer's personal spiritual life. I see biblical truth that intentionally represents and openly displays the plans and purposes of God. They are like scenes acted out on a stage, with God's intentions, and his strategy for his people. Even more crucially, how he works with us and how the individual believer, and the church, are meant to work together with him.

His plan is to seek out and to save the lost. His strategy is to use the church to accomplish this, and his strategies are clearly outlined and detailed in these biblical stories. That is why we have these stories. It is precisely why they are part of scripture. These stories, or accounts of events, to put it another way, are there not only to give an account of the life and ministry of Jesus and his miracles of two thousand years ago so that we might believe in him. Rather, they contain the very principles of the kingdom of God on earth and how he does things in order to achieve his purposes.

The outcome of the accounts outlined in this book of the wedding at Cana, the launching out into the deep, the feeding of the five thousand and the lame man carried on a stretcher by four friends, was always breakthrough, success, and abundance. It stands to reason that if the church today will capture the full essence of these events and simply apply them today, that we too will experience such phenomenal results. If doing things, with God, God's way, accomplished such great results then, surely doing them, with God, the same way today, will produce the same wonderful outcomes.

God, our loving Heavenly Father, had not committed to his church the responsibility for the great commission without having first openly demonstrated to us when he was here as one of us, by means of a series of what I refer to as life master-classes, just how to get the job done. I believe and indeed see that as he did things then, with obvious success, he will do the very same things now, with the same outcomes. In all of these bible accounts, Jesus was directly and personally involved. He was in the middle of every situation. He was coordinating events, and every situation always involved the active 'hands-on' participation of his disciples. That was the case then. Surely then it should and must also be the case today.

Confronted with this scene, which I am proposing dissatisfied and displeased Jesus, what was the very first thing he did? He simply got into one of the boats. What is the immediate lesson for us to learn here? It's this; in the midst of all the church's net washing activities today, Jesus wants to get on board our boats. But will we let him? The second action that Jesus took was to tell Peter to cast out a little from the land. Just a little. Just far enough, I think to perhaps remind Peter what a boat is designed for, and maybe also to remind Peter that a fisherman's life is served on the sea, not on the shore.

Equally for us today, the church's place of mission needs to be out there in the world, throughout society among the lost and not in the safe harbour of the shore.

Some years ago, during a church prayer time, a friend of mine saw a picture in his spirit of an aerial view of one of our beautiful local beaches. It was a happy scene of a beautiful day, with many hundreds of Christians having a barbecue beside the water. They were having a great time. Eating, chatting, singing, playing instruments, and so on. That's a great picture. I'm sure you'll agree. An interpretation was given, and that wasn't such a great picture. Through the interpretation, the Lord said, this is what my church is like. My people, blessed, having a wonderful time on the sandy shore under the beautiful blue sky, enjoying all of my blessings. But none of the fish in the sea right beside them were being in any way affected. The Lord said plainly; my people need to be in their boats, out on the water fishing for fish.

The third thing that Jesus did was that he began to teach the people from the boat which he was now sitting in. We see throughout the gospels that Jesus took every opportunity to gather a crowd wherever and whenever he could and then to teach them about God and his kingdom. I'll cover this more specifically in the next chapter on the feeding of the five thousand, where it says that when Jesus saw the multitudes, he was moved with compassion because they were faint and lost, just like sheep without a shepherd. And that he began to teach them many things. It is a fact that still today, God wants to teach us many things. And that he, throughout the scriptures, has so much to say to us regarding absolutely every conceivable aspect of life.

I believe, that there needs to be much more teaching in our churches on the work of the Great Commission - reaching out to the lost.

The church's ultimate focus should always be on how to win the lost. Each one of us who is saved was once ignorant about God and lost to the truth until someone approached us about Jesus, and we heard the gospel. Unfortunately, today most teaching and ministry seem to be aimed at the church. By that, I mean the focus is disproportionally aimed at blessing the Christian and helping, supporting, and encouraging the believer. That is all good, but not if that's where it ends. Jesus taught

- from the boat - to the people. His focus was on those that needed to hear his teaching, not on the crew of the boat. His teaching was outward, not inward.

I see in the New Testament that teaching to the church through the five-fold ministries outlined, for example, in Ephesians chapter four, is indeed aimed at the church. Teaching and ministry are specifically for the 'equipping of the saints for the work of ministry.' And what is the work of ministry? Is it to constantly teach over and over again with the aim of always encouraging and comforting the believer? No, it is ultimately to train the believer and equip the church - for the work of evangelism.

Something that has happened in this generation in the church is that believers are endlessly taught, endlessly encouraged, and endlessly comforted. But the work of evangelism has been neglected.

The church's true function has been marginalised, dissipated, and even lost to some extent. When we as leaders and pastors teach our congregations today, it should be from the perspective of us being on the water and reaching out to the lost. Not forever exhorting and constantly teaching those already saved, whist meanwhile hoping and praying that God will sovereignly and, independent of us, save the lost. That simply is not the biblical pattern. And in this particular scenario, Jesus is clearly and powerfully demonstrating that. In order to reinforce this point, let's take a look at the fourth thing that Jesus did. Verse four says, "Now when he had finished speaking, he said to Simon -launch out into the deep." So, Jesus had many things to say to those on the shore. He wanted to teach them many things from his position on the boat. But all he had to say to Simon Peter was a brief and curt instruction; "launch out into the deep."

To reemphasise the points above, teaching should always be followed by action. Or to put it another way, teaching should always be aimed towards creating action. Furthermore, teaching should always desire to expect action.

I personally believe that the church today has been taught to death. We see the principle of verse three here acted out with monotonous regularity each and every Sunday across the land. We see believers being taught over and over again. A seemingly endless stream of sermon after sermon, Sunday after Sunday, week in, week out, year in, year out. But the follow-through principle of verse four is all too often almost non-existent. The outcome is endless teaching but relatively very little launching out.

Here's my point; teaching doesn't catch fish. Only fishing catches fish. Teaching without launching out benefits only the church. It does absolutely nothing for the lost. Teaching without action is precisely what we are warned *not* to be; "hearers of the word but not doers."

Jesus didn't teach his sermon that day, then go home. I see a clear and intended principle in what he did. As in the other accounts of Jesus' ministry outlined in the various 'pictures' in this book, I see the outworking of how Jesus did things then and how the same Jesus still wants to do things today. Why should he model evangelism then and change his way of doing things today? Surely the living principles he demonstrated and outworked then, both with his disciples and with the multitudes, are the same principles that he would work out of today. He taught the multitude; then, he prompted his disciples into action.

Action should always follow teaching. And teaching should aim to stimulate and inform action.

What Jesus then said to Peter is at the very heart and substance of this story and the origins of my personal inspiration and revelation from these particular scriptures. Jesus didn't tell Peter he needed to pray for better results. Furthermore, he didn't even ask Peter why he hadn't been fishing but washing nets on the shore instead. He simply instructed him to launch out for a catch of fish. There are three distinct parts to this statement.

Launch out.
Into the deep.
For a catch of fish.

"Launch out." was a command, not a request. It was directive, not suggestive. It required deliberate action. It was directional, by that I mean it was going to take Peter from one place to another place, instantly. He was to 'launch out.' That is: Out from being static. Out of being inert. Out from the shoreline. Out from doing nothing to doing something. I could go on almost indefinitely, but the point I'm trying to make is that remaining where he was was no longer an option. Jesus had entered Peter's world. He had immediately changed his circumstances. He had gone into Peter's boat, possibly uninvited. He had made Peter move out a little bit onto the water. So he was gradually and incrementally, slowly but surely, moving Peter out from his inert and fruitless circumstances. Once on the water, Jesus did not then say, move out a little bit more, he commanded - launch out.

"Into the deep." God's purpose is to take each and every believer on a journey, a journey of faith and adventure, adventure into the world of mission, the world of impacting the multitudes. Furthermore, he does it by taking us out of our comfort zones. We are to walk by faith and not by sight. By his guidance, not our own. By his power and strength, not ours. By his strategies and plans and not our own. On a corporate level, by his strategies not by our ideas or church programmes. He wants to take us out into the deep. Like being in the deep end of a swimming pool when our feet don't touch the bottom. It is then the law of buoyancy applies. It's a matter then of sink or swim. But it's him who keeps us afloat. The deep is the *very opposite* of the shallows.

Christianity is meant to be outlived in the deep counsel of God, the deep revelation of the word of God, and the deep walk in the spirit of God.

"For a catch of fish." Here's the deal, Jesus knew where the fish were. He knew which fish were going to be caught that day. Today, God knows how to reach souls. He knows who is ready to be saved. He knows how to catch and land them. And he has unlimited strategies for doing the job. When the church falls in with what God is doing, success will follow. When we try to do it our way, it's just pot luck. This is evidenced by the fact that Jesus said launch out - *for a catch of fish*. Not might or maybe. You *will* catch fish. The church needs to rediscover that when we do God's work, God's way, and under God's direction, we are much more likely to achieve the results that God expects.

We are moving on now to verse five of this chapter. Peter's reply to Jesus instructing him to launch out into the deep is hugely significant. He said Master; we have toiled all night and taken (caught) nothing, nevertheless at your word I will let down (cast) the net.

Peter's response to Jesus is very revealing and is in two parts. I'll deal with the first part first:

"We have toiled all night and taken nothing." From this, we get a deeper and broader look into the picture that initially confronted Jesus when he saw the two ships standing by the lake with the fishermen out of them and washing their nets. That initial picture might suggest that the fishermen weren't even bothered about catching fish, preferring to dawdle about on the shore washing nets. We now discover that they had, in fact, been working very hard at their craft but had been unsuccessful. That they had "toiled all night" is a feature that just cannot be missed. I know very little about current commercial fishing and absolutely nothing about the methodology of fishing on the Sea of Galilee 2000 years ago. But I suspect that fishing through the night must have been a technique or perhaps even a tradition of fishermen in those times. Nevertheless, two things impact me:

They had quite literally - been 'working in the dark.' They had been fishing according to their own understanding, according to their 'traditions.' And it had proved fruitless.

We will discover by the end of this chapter that this entire story in the bible has absolutely nothing whatsoever to do with catching fish. Rather, it is a record of an event that took place, as a play, acted out in real-time by real people. This was performed for all people to see throughout the ages. And that this story, like so many others in the bible, serves to reveal the heart of God and to demonstrate just how he works, how he collaborates and partners with us, and what his methods and objectives are. Let's pause briefly to consider this thought: Here, we have a carpenter telling a seasoned professional fisherman - how to catch fish! Could there be more to this picture than meets the eye?

So, they had been working in the dark. So much Christian and church effort today is equally undertaken in the dark. Quite literally, a let's try this, let's try that approach. Like a stab in the dark, let's try this and see what happens. Then we wonder why it didn't work, why it produced little or no results, why nothing changed. Then like Peter, we get discouraged. Yes, discouraged. I think Peter's response to Jesus demonstrated a sense of discouragement, resignation to failure, of futility, perhaps even a sense of- what's the point of trying? He may well have been thinking; it's not that we haven't tried, we've been knocking our pan in all night. All night in the dark. There was no light in his sense of failure. No light in the futility he felt. No light in his understanding of why it hadn't worked or why they came up with nothing. He might also have been thinking, I can't understand why we caught no fish, why we were unsuccessful, after all, we have always done it this way, and it worked before.

Now here's the thing, either as individual Christians or church leaders, we can, with the very best of intentions and motives, get tied into the mentality that our traditions are right. That this is the way we have always done things, it worked before, why doesn't it work now? It's worth considering that Jesus didn't turn up whilst they were fishing in the dark during the night to bless their efforts and make them successful. No, he arrived at the dawn of a new day, during the daytime, quite literally - in the light, to show them how to do things. What am I saying here? I'm saying this: God simply will not bless our efforts, no matter how well-intended when they are based upon our own understanding of our church programmes or religious traditions. So often, we seek to achieve things in God, but it's based upon our own plans, our own personal, religious, or denominational understanding. Then we fervently knock ourselves out, praying that God will bless it. Then, all too often wonder why he didn't. Then, just like Peter, we also are left thinking - we have toiled all night and caught nothing.

I don't intend to pepper this book with hundreds of bible references, but I feel it's appropriate to give just a few at this point:

"Trust in the Lord with all your heart and lean not on your own understanding. In all your ways acknowledge him and he shall direct your paths."

"Unless the Lord builds the house, they labour in vain who build it."

"For we are God's fellow workers, you are God's field, you are God's building."

(Bible ref: Proverbs 3:5 / Psalm 127:1 / 1 Corinthians 3:9)

The second part of Peter's response to Jesus' command to launch out into the deep for a catch of fish is the truly exciting and 'revelatory' bit. Having said we have toiled all night and caught nothing (with all the negative connotations that represents), Peter added, "nevertheless at your word I will let down the net."

That statement, for me, is absolute dynamite. I simply cannot emphasise enough how utterly crucial it is for the believer today to grasp just what that statement represents and how it resonates and reverberates throughout the whole of the message of the Bible from Genesis to Revelation.

I would go as far as to say that the very point of me writing this book, the point of every word, every sentence, every paragraph, and every nuance is that I want to convey to the reader the cruciality, the wonder, the power, and the present and eternal significance and importance of that very significant statement; "Nevertheless, at your word."

Remember from the first chapter from the wedding at Cana, just before those serving at the feast were about to be instructed by Jesus to perform what initially seemed to be highly unusual, unorthodox, illogical and seemingly futile tasks; his mother said to them *whatsoever he says to you - do it.* This surely is meant to be the very essence of the spiritual walk in Christ. That is, *hearing from God* - then putting it into action.

- In the face of the unknown

- In the face of uncertainty

- In the face of the illogical

- In the face of the improbable

- In the face of fear

- In the face of terror

- In the face of failure

- In the face of defeat

- In the face of loneliness

- In the face of ignorance

- In the face of confusion

- In the face of sin

- In the face of sickness

- In the face of lack

- In the face of need - *Nevertheless, at your word!*

In fact, in the face of absolutely any situation, circumstance, fear, failure, or whatever we may each have to face in life, we are able to say to God - nevertheless, at your word. Particularly and specifically within the context of us serving God, of living out this spiritual life and in seeking to do the will of God in our lives, the message here is loud and clear.

You might now be thinking: Just what is it that is is so loud and clear? It is this:

We must personally and individually listen to and hear what Jesus says to us. We must get the 'now' word of God.

Peter must have been thinking; it doesn't make sense, I don't understand it, I can't see how it's going to work. I can't see how it's going to be any different than it was before. But Jesus, because you said it, I'm going to do it. But it's even more specific than that: Peter was saying because *you* said it, I'm going to do it. You see, Jesus walked into Peter's life, into his situation, into his world, into his challenges, into his specific and personal dilemma, then, whilst standing right beside him, he *spoke*. But more significantly, he spoke *personally and intimately* into Peter's ear!

Something I find that many believers seem to miss is the utter and absolute simplicity of just listening to what Jesus says and what he wants to say to them, personally, intimately and specifically. You see, in the midst of all this working in the dark, followed by routines of 'net washing,' we can miss the most fundamental and crucial element of our spiritual walk. We miss the revelation word of God. It's the revelation word of God that makes the difference.

And in times of need, confusion, and failure, it is *only* the revelation word of God that truly makes a real difference. I think the main lesson for us today is that like Peter and his fellow fishermen; we also can get caught up in a cycle of 'working all night and catching nothing.' I certainly know I have. Trying this and trying that to win souls. This programme and that programme. This outreach and that outreach. One special meeting with a special speaker followed by other special meetings and special speakers. But relatively little to show for it at the end of the day, or should I say - night. And such events being interspersed with long periods of net washing. In other words, routine bible studies, prayer meetings, and fellowship meetings, etc. So much so that like Peter, we at times feel disillusioned, despondent, and discouraged. The net washing can subtly become the norm. We think it's the way it's meant to be. It has become 'our tradition.' Meanwhile, for much of the time, the boats are tied up on the shore. We have come to believe that *this is the church*. Whilst it might indeed for some of us be an accurate reflection of what we now regard as church life; I earnestly believe that it's not how God intended it to be.

Jesus walked into Peter's situation and injected the one thing that was missing. *He spoke*. Peter got the message. We've tried everything and it's just not working. So now I'll do it your way. I'll do what *you say* to do. I'll follow *your word*. I'll listen to *your voice*, and I'll do what *you* tell me. *That* - I believe is the essence of doing things God's way. That is the essence of 'doing church' God's way. That is the essence of living the Christian life God's way. Otherwise we run the risk of achieving little more than a cyclical religious routine of washing nets on the shore of perpetual meetings of one kind or another. Week in, week out, with occasional results concerning church growth but generally not what we hope and pray for. So, are we wrong, have we failed? Of course not. But are we, like Peter and his fellow fishermen, stuck in a cycle of fruitlessness? Fruitlessness which is the result of pursuing circuitous, ineffective church routines, and religious traditions. Fruitlessness, which to some degree at least results from a lack of understanding on our part?

A lack of understanding that can be traced perhaps to the fact that many believers today quite simply aren't personally giving enough time and attention to the word of God. And as a result - not personally hearing from God to the extent that they should.

It took Jesus to get into Peter's boat and command him to launch out into the deep. But Peter had to be prepared to listen to him, then to act upon his words. What I'm attempting to say in this book is that the individual chapter subjects are each like a picture or a painting. That the content of the picture is the pure gold of biblical truth. And that this truth is perfectly and precisely framed. That each event depicted within the picture can be seen as a master-class, presented by Jesus himself, or even a play, with Jesus as the writer, producer, director, and lead actor. A play that represents a sort of specific snapshot of universal and eternal biblical truth. And that these pictures, plays, and snapshots are God's way of helping us, the individual believer and the collective church, to very clearly see, understand and learn, the principles and methods that he uses to accomplish his will and his purposes.

It can be extremely difficult to try to understand God and his will by attempting to plow through the entire bible. Let's face it, even the most diligent and impassioned Christians find that a daunting task. And even those who do can often come up with wrong or skewed conclusions. These scenarios, I believe, present us with pictures, 'painted' incidentally by the Master Painter, who, let us not forget, is both the author and the central figure of all the scriptures from Genesis to Revelation.

After all, who better to describe and explain any picture or painting than the artist himself?

So, for me, each of these pictures contains what I call highly concentrated truth. I have personally spent two-thirds of my life, around forty years, both studying and teaching the bible. I feel that I must add - and outworking it (quite clumsily for much of the time) throughout every aspect of my life and in my service to others, especially concerning the church.

I feel it would be quite impossible, for me to even attempt to broadly summarise the amazing strands and themes of wonderful truth and revelation contained within the pages of the bible. I find that they continually and increasingly blend together to form a huge tapestry. A tapestry that depicts a scene that portrays a picture. A picture that is so beautiful, so detailed, so comprehensive, and so complete. A finished picture but one that can be best understood by looking at a series of smaller pictures. Smaller pictures that deal with specific strands and threads that are snapshots of the complete and finished subject.

Paul wrote to Timothy, "Study to show yourself approved of God, a workman who need not be ashamed, rightly (or properly) dividing (or separating) the word of truth." In other words, dealing with parts of the big picture and separating out doctrine, breaking it down and presenting it in a way that can be more readily understood. The greatest example of this is, of course, the fact that Jesus spoke so much in parables. A parable is a short, natural, or practical story but with a spiritual meaning. Meaning which has profound depth but on the surface is presented in a simple yet condensed fashion. A spoken or written parable is, in fact, another example of a snapshot of truth. Just like 'apples of gold in pictures of silver.'

We have already looked at some of the elements or threads of spiritual truth which are contained within the account of Jesus instructing Peter to launch out into the deep. Now I want us to consider two more. The first is this: Jesus entered the initial scene of the fishermen washing their nets on the shore and the boats standing by the lake. He then worked his way into getting onto Peter's boat. In doing so, he was then personally working alongside Peter, and Peter was then working alongside him. So it had become a joint venture, a partnership, a collaboration. Prior to that, Peter knew Jesus and Jesus knew Peter. Just like being a Christian today. Just like being saved. If you are a saved person, you know Jesus, and he knows you. But Peter had been fishing without Jesus 'onboard.' It was having Jesus onboard that made all the difference.

The second thing I want to say here is that the most significant thing about having Jesus now onboard was that Jesus was now close enough to speak to Peter personally, intimately and specifically. Prior to that (in the night season), Peter was working alone and without guidance and instruction. Yes he knew Jesus and Jesus knew him. So it is with the Christian today. If we are truly saved, we can, with full assurance, say we know Jesus, and we know he knows us.

But have we personally allowed Jesus to come onboard concerning our calling, our spiritual walk, our Christian efforts, our ministry, and our church activities?

Have we personally heard his instruction to thrust out a little from the land? Away from the shoreline of self-effort and religious routines and traditions? Have we listened to his teaching?

Are we partnering with him, or are we working on our own? Have we personally and specifically heard his instructions to us? Have we experienced him being close enough to have our attention and our ear? Have we heard him commanding us to launch out into whatever 'deep' he is calling us to?

Because *that* is what made all the difference in Peter's life!

Real success and fruitfulness concerning the will and the purposes of God are not to be found on the safe and predictable shores of self-effort or religious traditions and predictable church routines.

- They are only to be found and experienced on the high seas of adventure.
- Adventure directed by Jesus himself.
- Adventure whereby we walk by faith and not by sight.
- Adventure whereby we are led by the Lord and not according to our own understanding.
- Adventure whereby we are doing what he has personally told us to do.
- Even when it flies in the face of convention, norms, or church or religious traditions.
- When it doesn't make much sense.
- When we don't understand the process.
- When we feel completely out of our depth.
- When we have doubts.
- When we are afraid.

Yet it is an adventure that has real security and assurance at its core. Security and assurance that we know that he is in the 'boat' with us. That we know we have heard his voice, personally and intimately. And that we possess a real sense of *knowing* what he has told us to do.

I think it's fair to say that sometimes it seems that our spiritual lives consist of mostly attending a seemingly never-ending cycle of one kind of meeting or another. Whether they are weekly prayer meetings, bible studies, the Sunday service and annual conferences, etc. Please don't misunderstand me. All of these things are great and we are very fortunate people indeed to have been spiritually called out of the sin-sickness and madness of this present world and to be able to enjoy the rich and wonderful ministry and fellowship of our local church communities and the wider kingdom of God. But if we are truly hoping to impact the lost all around us, we simply must not be satisfied unless these things lead to launching out.

Launching out takes us to places we have not been to before.

Places we may not understand.

Places where we might not feel comfortable.

Places where our instinct to play it safe is challenged.

Launching out takes away control from us and puts it firmly in the hands of God.

Launching out takes us far and away beyond the limitations of our own understanding.

It takes us much deeper into the realms of faith and obedience, risk, and self-sacrifice.

It takes us far deeper into truly trusting Jesus

Trusting him to the extent that our endeavours will be quite literally a case of sink or swim.

Surely it is very evident from all the scriptures from Genesis onwards and with respect to every significant character mentioned that the entire record of God's people is one of extreme adventure. Adventures about breaking out, breaking through, taking ground, fighting battles, overcoming impossible situations, gaining victories against overwhelming odds and pressing forward despite seemingly impossible obstacles.

The very first person mentioned in scripture to launch out, quite literally, was Noah. Absolutely everything that God had Noah do with his life flew in the face of convention, belief systems, world view, culture, and just about every other norm of the day. But Noah had heard from God. It was God who instructed him to build the ark. He not only told him to build it, but he gave him specific detailed instructions on how to do it.

Abraham launched out when he left his father's house to journey to an unknown land. In so doing, he embarked upon a journey, the significance of which was totally beyond his comprehension. But it was God who told him to do it. Moses launched out from a mundane life of tending sheep in the backside of the desert. A life incidentally which the bible tells us he was content with, into an adventure beyond his wildest dreams. He was later to literally launch out into the Red Sea, taking around six hundred thousand people with him. I could, of course, go on to speak about Joshua, David, Gideon, and so many others. It was Jesus who entered Peter's life, spoke personally and specifically to him, and caused him to launch out. The bible says that Jesus Christ is the same yesterday today and forever. What Jesus did with Peter was a continuation of what God has always done with his people. He calls them into partnership with himself then leads them on an extraordinary journey. And what Jesus did with Peter, he wants to do with you and me today. Washing nets on the shore are symbolic of a mundane life. A predictable life. A life that essentially revolves around one's self. A life that is limited to one's abilities and restricted by one's personal limitations. Launching out into the deep is symbolic of life entirely reliant upon God. Reliant upon God for instruction. Reliant upon God for direction. Reliant upon God for understanding. And reliant upon God's power and ability, not our own.

Here is just some idea of the extent to which the "deep" part of God's instruction to "launch out" refers to. What we cannot comprehend naturally, but what I understand to be true is that like Noah, Abraham, Moses, and so many other bible characters, we simply do not know just how much impact our willingness and obedience to launch out will have in the lives of others. Or how it will shape and advance the church and the kingdom of God both now and into the future.

Had they not been receptive to the voice of God and his personal instructions and directions to them, Noah and his family would have drowned in the flood along with everyone else.

Abraham would have lived out the rest of his ordinary life with his fellow-countrymen within a culture of idolatry in Ur, perpetuating the culture, traditions and beliefs of his fathers.

Moses would have lived out his life as an unknown shepherd, quite oblivious to the extraordinary and phenomenal purpose and calling God had for him. However, they did listen. They did obey. And they did launch out. The rest, as they say, is history. But we may ask ourselves, what relevance has that for me as a Christian today? Well, I think that depends on whether we believe what's written in the bible or not. Here are just a few relevant verses from the New Testament:

"For we are His workmanship, created in Christ Jesus for good works, which God prepared beforehand that we should walk in them."

"I therefore, the prisoner of the Lord beseech you to walk worthy of the calling with which you are called."

"I beseech you therefore brethren, by the mercies of God, that you present your bodies a living sacrifice, holy, acceptable to God, which is your reasonable service."

Jesus teaches us to seek *first* the kingdom of God and his righteousness (that which is right for him or right in his eyes.)

In the Lord's Prayer, he instructs us to pray - Let your will be done on earth as it is in heaven. That prayer, of course, means; show *me* how to do *your* will during my life here on earth. *(Bible Ref: Ephesians 2:10 / Ephesians 4:1 / Romans 12:1 / Matthew 6:9)*

So very much depends upon us understanding the will of God on how much we expose ourselves to the word of God.

We considered previously that Peter had toiled all night and caught nothing. And that the difference the following day was that Jesus was now on board his vessel and was telling him what to do. This is an example of the Christian labouring in the kingdom but without sufficient instruction and guidance. The voice of God then is the same as the voice of God now. Jesus speaks today the same today as he spoke then. He seeks to get up close and personal with us today, in the same way, he got up close and personal with Peter then.

He wants to encourage us to "thrust out a little from the land" now as he did then.

He wants to "teach from within the boat" now the same as he taught from within the boat then.

He wants to speak personally into our ears from a place of closeness now as he did then.

It is then, and I believe and only then, that we are ready to hear him say "launch out into the deep." And it is only then that we can personally understand what that means.

The crucial thing here is *hearing* what God has to say to us - personally. Or to put it another way, for him to speak directly and specifically into our lives. It is not uncommon today for us as believers to hear hundreds of Sunday sermons but still not know what God requires of us. To attend weekly bible studies over many years but still not have much of a grasp of what the bible is all about. To faithfully attend regular prayer meetings but still not really know the will of God for our lives. That's because we can indeed faithfully do all of those things, which in many ways are rightly an outward expression of our faith, but which, over time, can become little more than a repetitive routine. Whilst doing those worthy things, it is possible to neglect personally spending real time alone with God. Such a Christian lifestyle can, over time, amount to little more than 'washing nets.'

- *Perpetual weekly sermons but relatively little personal serving.*

- *Perpetual weekly bible studies but little personal internal impact or change.*

- *Perpetual prayer meetings but with no specific objectives or outcomes.*

- *In other words, constant net washing but little or no launching out.*

Such a Christian life really doesn't demand much of a person. It is safe, secure, predictable, and comfortable. But it produces few results and very little personal spiritual growth or maturity. Such a pattern over time can lead to a religious life which is static and circuitous.

In many ways, it resembles the life of the Israelites who wandered in the wilderness, repeatedly covering the same ground for forty years because they failed to 'launch out' into the promised land under Moses. That generation spent forty years 'washing nets' until a new generation led by Joshua did launch out. They launched out of the wilderness, across the river Jordan and into Canaan, the promised land. Into a new land. A land of battles, victories, advancement, growth, possession, fruitfulness, and success. A land of adventure. A land in which, unlike their forty years in the wilderness, they were fulfilling the will of God. To put it even more plainly, they were *doing* what they were called to do.

To understand biblical things, we have to see them from a biblical perspective. It is my personal view that the account of Jesus instructing Peter to launch out into the deep is one of a number of examples that demonstrate how God works, how he does things, and, more specifically, how he works and operates, both with individuals and within the church. The church let us not forget it is 'his body.' As members of his body, we should each be doing what he wants us to do. And that body, like a human body, is governed by the head. Jesus is the head of the church. Spiritually speaking, he does the thinking, the planning, and the coordination. All we have to do is take instructions from him.

Furthermore, as I also outline in the other examples offered in this book, I believe that if that is how Jesus did things then, that is how he still does them. Let me explain: Why should Jesus do all that he did then, as recorded in the four gospels, now do things differently today? If that's how he engaged with his disciples, then why would he engage with them differently now? If that is how he operated in the midst of his church (those whom he calls) then, why would he operate any differently today? Why would he present or 'stage' all these profound and wonderful examples then, at the very laying of the foundation of the church, then decide not to apply them today? Yet you would sometimes think that this is indeed the case.

Many Christians today have very little understanding of how the Bible applies to them or what God wants to achieve both within them and through them.

Here's another thought: Throughout the Old Testament, God provided his people with thoroughly intricate and specific details and instructions concerning such things as:

- The building of Noah's Ark.
- The Tabernacle in the wilderness.
- The Ark of the Covenant.
- The function of the priests.
- The division of the tribes.
- Levitical law.
- The building plans for the building of Solomon's temple.

Furthermore, he commanded his people to obey his specific directions and instructions and not to deviate from them, disobey them, or forget them. They were repeatedly told and constantly reminded that their success or failure, victory or defeat, fruitfulness or barrenness, was determined entirely on their adherence and obedience to the word of God. Not just the written word of God but the revelation word of God. Revealed to them specifically for their personal lives and for the times in which they lived. But the people of the Old Testament were not merely required to listen to God's word, to learn God's word, and to know God's word, they were also required to *do* it, to apply it and to walk it out. Also consider this: the Old Testament was to pass away. The Tabernacle, the Ark of the Covenant, the Priesthood, and Solomon's Temple were to all pass away. All of those things were the foundation, the preparation and the prelude to the greatest event of all;

The coming of the Messiah and the birth of the church.

The church, which was to become the spiritual Ark which would gather in countless millions of people over the ages.

The church whose members would become the spiritual Priesthood.

The church which would become God's spiritual Temple on earth.

The church which would become the recipients and ministers not of Levitical Law but of the law of Grace, the law of the New Covenant.

The church through which souls would be saved for all of eternity.

Is it conceivable that God would provide so much clarity, so much information and such detailed and specific attention in the Old Testament, to design for that which was foundational but to pass away, but leave the church which was to be the culmination of all of those things and which was to have permanent and eternal significance, to sort of figure things out for themselves? Of course not! The key to success for the New Testament Church is exactly the same as the key to success was for the Old Testament Saints - namely, hearing and obeying the voice of God. Moses' generation was too afraid to obey God's voice. They 'stayed on the shore' and quite literally went round in circles all of their lives. Joshua's generation, 'launched out' across Jordan, into the promised land and into everything that God had prepared for them to possess and accomplish.

This is what God said to Joshua "Moses my servant is dead. Now therefore arise, go over this Jordan, you and all this people, to the land which I am giving to them - the children of Israel." God also promised success and victory in all they did and that he would always be right there with them. Right there beside them. Just like Jesus did in the boat with Peter. But there was a clear condition to those promises; "Only be strong and very courageous, that you may observe to do according to all the law which Moses, my servant commanded you. Do not turn from it to the right hand or to the left, that you may prosper wherever you go." *(Bible ref: Joshua 1:2 / 1:7)*

Peter said: "Lord, we have toiled all night and caught nothing, nevertheless - at your word."

There it is. There we have it. That's it. That's the secret. That's the pattern. That's the plan. That's how this all works. That's how this Christian life works. That's how the church is meant to work. Jesus in the New Testament is - quite literally - the Personification of the Word of God. And if he is in our 'boat' right there with us, speaking to us, directing us, working alongside us - just how can we fail to succeed?

So, upon hearing Jesus' instructions (his word), Peter let down the net. This is then what happened: "And when they had done this they enclosed a great multitude of fishes, and their nets broke. And they called unto their partners who were in the other ship for them to come and help them. And they came, and they filled both ships so full that they began to sink." What a turn around.

What a different picture from the one at the start of the day. In such a short space of time, they had gone from having nothing - to having too much. From having no fish - to having more than they could handle. From washing nets - to those same nets now bursting with fish. From lack - to abundance. From failure - to success. From empty boats - to boats so full they were sinking. And, dear church, we simply cannot afford to miss this: from lone fishing - to calling upon other fishermen to help them. From working separately - to working together.

So let's now summarise what it was that brought such dramatic change and consider what it means for the individual believer and the church today:

- Jesus personally entered the scene.

- They quit washing nets.

- They let Jesus come onboard.

- They cast out a little and onto the water (where they belonged).

- They listened to him teaching.

- They facilitated that teaching outward - towards the people.

- They listened to what Jesus told them personally.

- The acted on his 'specific and situation based' instructions.

- They got his 'word' for their situation.

- They 'launched out' - on *that* word.

- The did things his way, not their own way.

We learn then that they were astonished at what had just happened. They also had shifted dramatically from despondency to astonishment. Surely that will be the same for us when we do God's work God's way. Jesus then said to them, "From now on, you shall catch men." So *that's* what this 'masterclass' was all about. Seeing and experiencing first hand, at the hand of the Master, the spiritual principles, and the spiritual process for the successful and over-abundant catching, not of fish, but men. The work of evangelism. The work of *every* believer. The work of the church. This picture closes with the most amazingly clear announcement. An announcement that demonstrates with crystal clarity the real meaning behind this remarkable event which occurred within the opening chapters of the gospels: "And when they had brought their ships to land (and of course all the fish), they forsook it all and followed Jesus." And all of this had - *absolutely nothing* - to do with fish!

Footnote:

Although the main themes of this book are generally about the church, kingdom, Christian service, and evangelism, I feel I should just briefly state that all biblical truth, of course, can and should apply to every aspect of the believer's life. We are instructed by God to "acknowledge him in all of our ways." Furthermore, from Genesis onwards, all of God's people throughout the bible are directed to listen to his word and put it first in their lives. The promises being that if we do, we will be led by him, our path will be straight, we will walk in the light, we will be fruitful, and we will have good success. The concept of launching out into the deep can equally apply to any aspect of our lives, from jobs, career choices, finances, personal decisions, and relationships, etc. It is essentially about allowing God to lead and guide us - and consulting him when we should. But it is, I believe, primarily about the disciple of Jesus, allowing him to take us beyond our natural limitations and beyond our understanding so that we can fulfill God's calling on our lives.

Chapter Four

Feeding of Five Thousand

(Blueprint of the Church)

Gospel of Mark. Chapter 6: 30-44

[30]Then the apostles gathered to Jesus and told Him all things, both what they had done and what they had taught. [31]And He said to them, "Come aside by yourselves to a deserted place and rest a while." For there were many coming and going, and they did not even have time to eat. [32]So they departed to a deserted place in the boat by themselves.

[33]But the multitudes saw them departing, and many knew Him and ran there on foot from all the cities. They arrived before them and came together to Him. [34]And Jesus, when He came out, saw a great multitude and was moved with compassion for them, because they were like sheep not having a shepherd. So He began to teach them many things. [35]When the day was now far spent, His disciples came to Him and said, "This is a deserted place, and already the hour is late. [36]Send them away, that they may go into the surrounding country and villages and buy themselves bread; for they have nothing to eat."

[37]But He answered and said to them, "You give them something to eat." And they said to Him, "Shall we go and buy two hundred denarii worth of bread and give them something to eat?"

[38]But He said to them, "How many loaves do you have? Go and see." And when they found out they said, "Five, and two fish." [39]Then He commanded them to make them all sit down in groups on the green

grass. ⁴⁰So they sat down in ranks, in hundreds and in fifties. ⁴¹And when He had taken the five loaves and the two fish, He looked up to heaven, blessed and broke the loaves, and gave them to His disciples to set before them; and the two fish He divided among them all.

⁴²So they all ate and were filled. ⁴³And they took up twelve baskets full of fragments and of the fish. ⁴⁴Now those who had eaten the loaves were about five thousand men.

So here we are now at picture four. It has certain very clear similarities to pictures two and three, namely, Jesus is again with his disciples. Again, there is need. Again, he has dialogue with them. Again, he gives them instructions. In other words, he tells them what to do. Like the two previous scenarios, what he tells them to do doesn't appear to make much sense. And again, and it is very important for the Christian to hear this, *he engages them fully in the process.* Again, it is a partnership and again it requires their direct involvement and their actions. In other words, they don't just ask Jesus to do something, to fix the problem, to supply the needs, he then does it and everyone goes home happy.

So, we immediately see a very major difference between that scenario and the kind of thinking that suggests we are to simply ask God to do things then sit back and expect him to deliver.

I see the feeding of the five thousand as another 'real life workshop' or 'masterclass' led by Jesus to demonstrate how he operates. And what our (his 21st century disciples) role in that is. So let's break this narrative down into five sections.

1. The Multitude

2. Jesus'Response

3. The Disciples Response

4. Jesus Commands Action

5. The Plan Put Into Action

Section 1 - The Multitude

When Jesus saw the multitudes of people, he was moved with compassion towards them, because they were as sheep not having a shepherd.

Being moved with compassion for people was the heart of God then, and it remains the heart of God today. It is a common occurrence in the gospels that when

Jesus saw the multitudes that he was moved with compassion. One other example of many is in Matthew 9:36, which says: *"But when he saw the multitudes, he was moved with compassion for them, because they were weary and scattered, like sheep having no shepherd."*

Jesus' heart ached for all those people, all those strangers, all those men, women, and children. He felt sorry for them, he felt anxious for them, he was worried about them, and he was fearful for them and their future. Why? Because he saw that they were all hungry, all physically weak, all unable to meet their own essential needs. All without someone to take care of them, feed them, lead, guide, and organise them, just like a flock of sheep. All individuals, wandering about. All having such great need but not knowing what to do about it. Isn't that just like society today?

Isn't it just the same today as it was then? Yes, we are more sophisticated, more knowledgeable, better educated, more structured politically and socially, much more technologically advanced, and so on. Yet the core human condition remains the same. People are hungry for something, but they don't know what. They seek to fill this hunger with all sorts of things. They get tired and weary with all the pressures and worries of life. But even more crucially, the vast majority of people, if they are honest and take the time to think about it, really don't know where they are going. What they are really doing, what life is truly all about, where they are heading, how it will end? Then, what is the end? Is it the end? What's the purpose of it all? Is there a God? And if there is a God, who is he, what is he like? Where is he? And what has it all got to do with me anyway?

Section 2 - Jesus' Response - Teach Them Many Things

What happens next simply astounded me when I first saw it. When I say I first saw it, I don't mean when I first read it. I had been familiar with this text for many years and had read it many times. Indeed, I had taught from it on many occasions.

But one day, about fifteen years ago, the revelation of the entire story about the feeding of the five thousand just fell on me. That's the best way I can describe it. It simply fell on me. I might have been gardening at the time or doing housework. And this all just suddenly became clear. But let me explain something. By God's grace alone, I am a diligent and studious bible reader. I have been since I became a Christian in 1975. At that time, at the age of twenty-three, I heard the gospel preached for the very first time. It changed me profoundly, absolutely, on the spot. On the inside, in my heart, in my mind, and my very being. That story is for another time. The point is this, the preacher at the time was preaching from the bible. He was preaching the words of Jesus. And when I heard and received the words of Jesus, my whole life was phenomenally impacted. Impacted for the better in every conceivable sense. From day one, I was drawn to the bible, the scriptures, the Word of God. I had (quite unwittingly at that point) become a disciple of Jesus. I joined a church, got to know lots of other Christians, and began an incredible journey of life-long learning - and service!

Throughout the gospels, Jesus taught his disciples (and, of course, still does today) to "seek first the kingdom of God." That is, to make an ongoing inquiry about him, his ways, and his will for their lives. And to always make that the number one priority in their lives. He teaches that the person who seeks will find. To the person who knocks doors will be opened. And the person who diligently asks will receive. All this refers to seeking knowledge, wisdom, and understanding, and of course, to understand the will of God for our lives. The opposite is naturally applicable. If a person doesn't ask, doesn't seek, and doesn't knock, they won't receive these things. The bible teaches that God will pour water on those who are thirsty. That is, thirsty for knowledge, thirsty for truth, thirsty for God, and for more of God.

This all amounts to a person understanding more about God. Understanding more about themselves. Understanding more about others. Understanding more about life and what it is all about. The core questions, why are we here? Where did we come from? What is life's purpose? Who am I? What is wrong with the world? Why is there so much sorrow? Why do such terrible things happen? Where is God in all of this?

The reason Jesus felt such compassion for the multitudes was because he knew then and still knows now that they were and still are, going through life blind and afraid and confused and insecure and lost and lonely. Even though they were in a crowd of five thousand people, each was still an individual. An individual who carries all of these feelings, emotions, and concerns. And each one of us is still the same today.

But getting back to my explanation about this "revelation," or to put it another way, this sudden profound clarity. I believe and understand this; it is precisely because I had for many years sought and asked and knocked and thirsted for answers, that God was faithful to his promises. He gave me (to some extent) what I'd been looking for; knowledge and understanding.

Knowledge and understanding about what? About his kingdom, here on earth. About his church and what it's for. About his people, what they should be doing, and how they should do it. About me and my place in all of that.

So, what was it that astounded me? It was this; faced with that sea of human need, Jesus didn't simply, miraculously, with a wave of his hand, create food enough for five thousand people. Though no doubt he most certainly could have. Surely that would have been enough to demonstrate or prove who he was if indeed that was his intention - to perform a miracle to demonstrate his power and his divinity. If the biblical account of the feeding of the five thousand was just a miracle to demonstrate these things (as many people believe), he would have done it there and then. But he didn't. Instead, this is what he did: "He began to teach them many things."

The misery that Jesus saw before him was not merely temporary physical hunger - It was a chronic and profound spiritual need.

Jesus knew that them being faint and scattered abroad (isolated) and like sheep without a shepherd (with no real direction in life) was because of what they *didn't know*. In other words, because of their ignorance. More specifically, because of their ignorance about God.

We don't know how long Jesus spoke on this occasion; the bible doesn't say. But if he "began to teach them many things," it must have been quite a long time. Just think about trying to explain any new subject to someone else. A subject they previously knew absolutely nothing about. You'd have to start from scratch, build it up gradually, then get into the details. That alone could take quite some time. On this occasion, Jesus did precisely that but about "many things." How many things we don't know? But we should have a good idea what some of those many things were. They would no doubt have been some of the many parables, stories, and other teachings that he taught throughout his three-year ministry. All of which are recorded in the gospels.

What is very evident is that Jesus put the people's spiritual needs before their physical needs because even though he knew they were hungry, he spent considerable time teaching them first.

The thing that is staring us in the face here is this: Physical hunger is a daily reality. We get hungry, and we eat food several times a day. Natural food fulfills the needs of the physical body. But only spiritual food can meet the needs of the spiritual dimension of our lives. And that spiritual food is the word of God. And the word of God is contained in the person of Jesus.

I'll mention this here but not elaborate upon it as it would take us away from the focus of this chapter. The scripture here says, - he *began* to teach them many things. I believe that it is very, very significant. Jesus, in person, began to teach the multitudes many things. It is for the church today to *continue* what he started. That is, to comprehensively and thoroughly teach the many "things" of the full counsel of the word of God. Not just part of the word of God alongside a whole lot of church traditions, Christian cliches, and doctrinal biases. If the church today isn't all it should be, I personally believe it is precisely for this very reason.

Section 3 - The Disciples Response - Send Them Away

When Jesus finished teaching the people, his disciples came to him and said, "This is a desert place, and now the time is far passed. Send them away so they may go into the country round about and into the villages to buy themselves bread, for they have nothing to eat."

This is the second thing that struck me. Here are his twelve disciples and five thousand tired, needy, hungry people. The disciples are aware that this is a problem. To put it one way, they were thinking; there's too many of them and not enough of us. There are far too many mouths to feed, and we certainly don't have enough, if indeed any, food. So they applied natural logic to a natural problem. They had concluded that everyone should go their own way and take care of themselves.

Their conclusion was to tell Jesus to "send them away." Just like that, problem solved. The thinking essentially being, it's not our problem. Of course, the disciple's viewpoint is perfectly understandable. They weren't being insensitive or lacking in compassion; they simply saw the situation to be too big to possibly have anything to do with them.

But remember, I said earlier, I believe this entire event was a real-time workshop, a masterclass, by the master. A masterclass, a learning on-the-job for the disciples in what he was all about, how he did things, and, more importantly - how it involved *them.*

My professional background was for many years as manager of a regional social work crisis and emergency response team. I was out of the office on one occasion when I received a call from a member of my team. She was a highly qualified, excellent practitioner but new to front-line crisis work. She was alone in the office and was dealing with several new referrals at the same time, which in that line of work was not uncommon. To top it all, she was having to deal with a belligerent and demanding Police Inspector on the phone.

She told me she found him intimidating and said she felt overwhelmed. She stressed that she felt she needed assertiveness training. Knowing her as I did and having personally taken her through induction training for the job, which included in the field joint-working, I replied: "Anne, that is precisely what you are doing right now - assertiveness training."

She got the message, and we laughed about it later. The fact is, she learned more and honed her skills faster, through that one experience, that one encounter, than she would have done at any week-long Assertiveness Training Course.

After all, crisis management, which by its very nature frequently involved dealing with hostility and confrontation, is what the job entailed. It's 'what we did.'

That is precisely what was happening here with Jesus' disciples. He was teaching them, demonstrating to them - in the field and on the job. He was showing them what the job entailed. He was showing them - 'what he did," More importantly, he was showing them what *their* job was. And he was about to demonstrate to them that like Anne, they already possessed the skills, the personal resources, and the capacity to do it.

No more courses, no more qualifications, and no more specialist training. This was it; hands-on, learn as you go but more crucially, learn as you *do*.

I'm sure you'll appreciate that I'm attempting to parallel all of this with the here and now. The church today. The Christian today. If so, then let me point this out:

It wasn't just the multitude that heard his teaching; it was also his disciples. You will find many times throughout the gospels that when Jesus taught the crowds of people about say, the parable of the sower or the sermon on the mount, etc., that he followed that by taking his disciples aside later to explain the meaning of what he had just taught the crowds. This would have been no different.

Furthermore, so often in the gospels (as demonstrated in chapters two and three of this book), Jesus' teaching is immediately followed by action. Quite literally, the practical application of what he had just taught.

Now here's a 21st-century problem: Christianity and church life these days is all too often characterised by seemingly endless teaching - but comparatively little personal application, follow-through, or action.

It's all too common these days for believers to attend church and other meetings to hear sermon after sermon, sermon upon sermon, week after week, month after month, year in year out. It seems that we have come to regard this as normal. That is what many consider what it means to be a Christian and to live a Christian life. To go to church, hear a message, decide whether or not it was a good one, whether or not it 'spoke' to us, go home, then go back to church the following week for more of the same. Midweek meetings of all varieties or other special meetings, large or small, almost invariably amount to the same. It seems to be the norm that the believer's expectation is that they go to church or other gatherings to hear a message that might encourage them.

And that the role of the pastor or minister is to encourage, comfort and inspire the flock. And that they do so by perpetual bible teaching or the preaching of sermons.

However, this is not the biblical model of Christianity or of the church. Constant exposure to *just* teaching of any kind, not just bible teaching, but without personal or practical application, achieves little. It merely results in people who may have stored up information they have received from others, but it neither truly impacts them or those around them.

Consider again Anne, who I mentioned before. Had she not applied her specialist knowledge and training to the real-life challenge that faced her, she might never have overcome her sense of fear and feelings of weakness and intimidation.

No amount of further teaching or specialist courses would have equipped her the way that on-the-job experience did. All she would have achieved was more information but no change or personal growth within herself and no impact on those around her, just like the Christian hearing yet another sermon. Anne had to apply and 'work through' what she had already previously learned. She had to apply her knowledge and her training to real-life situations. It was only by *doing* that she discovered the knowledge and skills that she possessed. It was only by *doing* that all she had previously learned became an actual reality. By phoning me, Anne was, in a sense telling me to 'send it away' that the problem was too big for her and should be dealt with by someone else. Of course, I could have stepped in, taken over, and resolved that difficult situation. But had I done so, she wouldn't have crossed that threshold between merely knowing and doing. Her practice as a crisis manager wouldn't have developed, and she would have continued to doubt her abilities.

What happens next in this account of the feeding of the five thousand demonstrates this point very clearly.

Section 4 - Jesus Commands Action

So the disciples looked at the situation before them, thought about it, then figured it was too big for them. They then concluded that the solution lay somewhere else or with someone else. Precisely the same very often applies today in churches and the individual Christian's life. We look at people's needs all around us. We look at the state of the world, of society and we think, too big a problem, too much for us. It might be that we think the answer is in having outreaches, conventions, gospel campaigns, and the like. All of which is good and commendable. But even at that, it's still a kind of 'send them away.' Some Christians believe that praying for revival will do the job. That, too, is good and commendable. But it is also a kind of 'send them away' - the solution lies elsewhere, it's outwith our scope. But it's not how Jesus saw the problem. It's not how he saw the solution, either.

It is worthy of note that Jesus didn't discuss his disciple's views or enter into debate with them. He didn't even answer them. He ignored what they said and simply commanded, "You feed them." That was it. After all their deliberations amongst themselves. After all the thought they had given to the situation. After they had come up with a plan. Is that not sometimes like the church today? With the very best of intentions and with absolute sincerity, we think things through, thoroughly discuss them, come up with a plan, then 'tell Jesus what to do.' That is, we pray that God will facilitate and bless our efforts. It's little wonder then why he seems to ignore what we said (generally perceived by us as God not answering our prayers). I think Jesus simply does with us (his disciples) now, as he did with his disciples then. He lets us pour out our concerns, our fears, our doubts, and then our conclusions, to him in prayer. He then doesn't engage us at that level - but says (throughout his word). "You do it."

But, do what exactly, I hear you say? They asked precisely the same question. They asked Jesus, "shall we go and buy two hundred pennyworths of bread and give them to eat?"

This is now the second time the disciples applied their natural logic to what was, in fact, a spiritual problem. The first time was when they said to send them away. Now they were asking, do you want us to go and buy enough food to feed them all?

Though they didn't understand it yet, they had entered into this situation, thinking it was all about actual, natural, physical food. They were applying natural human logic to the problem and understandably, coming up with natural, logical conclusions and solutions, or at least trying to. But Jesus was engaging them in 'on-the-job' understanding of:

- What the real needs were.

- How God sees human need.

- God's priorities regarding those needs.

- How God meets those needs.

- How he uses his disciples (us) and the church in meeting those needs.

- How the church works.

- How his kingdom advances.

What I'm proposing is that this event, the principles contained within it and the lessons to be learned from it, represent a template, a blueprint, I would go as far as to say; *The Blueprint*, of how the individual Christian and the church collectively are designed to function. It has always struck me that in the Old Testament how God gave commands and directions to his people (Just as Jesus was doing in this situation) but that he also gave them the plan and the design as to how to do what he was telling them. For example, he told Noah to build an ark, which, as we know, was a type of foreshadowing of the church, inasmuch that it was designed to lift men and women above the waves of God's impending judgment. But he also gave Noah the detailed design of *how* to build it, what materials to build it with, and all its measurements and dimensions.

God instructed Moses to build the Tabernacle in the wilderness. But in doing so, he also gave him precise details about its dimensions, its compartments, all the materials and fabrics for its construction, and the vessels and equipment to be used within it. The same applied to God's intricately detailed plans that he gave to King David for the temple at Jerusalem that his son Solomon was later to have built. Built-in accordance with those plans. In accordance with that 'blueprint.' Yet, very often, when we consider how we think as Christians and how we 'do church' that when it comes to the New Testament Church, which is after all the fulfillment and the culmination of all those things that went before and which were to pass away - that God gave no clear plan, no blueprint. That how the Church is meant to operate and how the Christian is supposed to function within it, has to all intents and purposes been left to chance. And that we somehow have to figure it out for ourselves.

Let's make something very clear, crystal clear in fact before we move on. I'm sure that every Christian will agree that something which is wonderfully and perfectly clear throughout the pages of the bible is that all men and women everywhere need to repent. That they need to accept Christ as Saviour. They need to receive the free gift of salvation. They can then receive the person of the Holy Spirit who can empower them to live a victorious, holy, and fruitful life in service to Jesus, our Lord and Saviour. Yes, all that, I'm sure we all agree, is wonderfully clear.

It's what happens after that, which is often not so clear. In fact, for many Christians today, not clear at all. Which church should I attend, or what is the right church for me? These are questions so often asked by many believers. Questions that some very sadly never seem to resolve. Others feel they have been 'hurt' in church or take offense at something and withdraw from active fellowship.

Some tragically eventually grow cold and fall away from the faith.

The problem, I believe, is that believers can become 'disillusioned' with the church, essentially because they have never really understood what church is meant to be. They are disillusioned because they have a mistaken illusion of what the Church of Jesus is in the first place.

I can understand when believers go through such things because I am of the opinion that the bible has not been taught as fully and as comprehensively as it should be. There has and still is, in my personal opinion, far too much emphasis on 'attending meetings' and far too little emphasis on personal discipleship, personal responsibility, personal spiritual growth, and crucially - *the believers, purpose, function and service* within the kingdom of God. It is those things that lead Christians into spiritual maturity and which enable them to understand their place, their purpose, and their function within the local church and the wider body. During my early years as a Christian, I wrestled with the issue of which church to attend and with trying to find out where I belonged and fitted in. I have since learned it's not which church you attend that matters, but where you can best serve within the body of Christ. That requires an understanding of how the 'body' works and how the believer finds their place of service and ministry within it. When the believer begins to understand that, it casts an entirely different light on the whole issue of church. It is said that 'identity precedes function.' A major issue is that very many Christians do not know their identity within the body of Christ. They *cannot* therefore function' as they should. That then detracts from the church community.

Jesus firmly criticised religious traditions in his time. And I think there is scope for us to beware of religious traditions in our own life and times. Much of Jesus' criticism of religious tradition was aimed at practices that developed over time and which had gradually become more important than what is contained in the scriptures. He said that the "tradition of men" made the word of God "of none effect." So what 'traditions' are we faced with today? One current widespread and entrenched tradition can be summed up as follows:

The believer 'goes to' church. The pastor, the minister, teaches/preaches the word of God to the congregation. This is repeated every week - ad-infinitum.

This cyclical pattern, this 'Christian culture,' has become a tradition. It has become *our* tradition. To put it another way; It's traditionally how we do things. It's traditionally how we 'do church.' And it is generally considered to be the lifestyle of the average Christian today. So, as the Jews had their traditions in Jesus' time, so the church has its traditions today.

There is always the danger of yesterday's traditions becoming today's truth. And - for today's traditions to become tomorrow's truth. That is a challenge for every generation, including ours. I personally and firmly believe it should be a real and present challenge for every church leader and every Christian today. After all, we are called and commanded by God to "walk in the truth." How can we walk in the truth unless we know what the actual truth is?

So let's get back to the text. Remember, this is an event in the life of Jesus 'working with' his disciples. An event that we are portraying as a picture. A picture that paints a thousand words. Words in this case, which I believe, capture in a single event, the very essence, in condensed form, of fundamental New Testament truth.

I would go as far as to say that if we can truly grasp the clear and simple spiritual principles portrayed within this single event; the feeding of the five thousand, that the pages of the whole of the New Testament will become significantly clearer to us. Especially concerning our understanding about the church. And of equal importance - our role in it!

Let's briefly recap:

- *Jesus saw the great needs of the multitude*

- *He was moved with compassion*

- *He 'began' to teach them many things*

- *Then, because it was getting late, and the people were hungry, the disciples told Jesus to send them away.*

- *Jesus replied by simply saying: You feed them!*

- *Just like that. No deliberations, no debate, no explanations, and absolutely no hesitation.*

- *He was in effect saying:*

- *You don't need to send them away; you can deal with this yourselves.*

- *You have the resources amongst yourselves to meet this need.*

- *The answer to this need lies within you.*

We see throughout the gospels that when Jesus spoke to the crowds wherever he went, he always spoke to them in parables. The bible says that he never spoke to the crowds unless it was in parables. But afterward, privately, he would explain to his disciples what the parable meant. A parable, as we know, is a natural story with a spiritual meaning. This was no different. The feeding of the five thousand, rather than being a natural story with a spiritual meaning, was a natural 'event' but with a spiritual meaning. The natural element of the event was feeding very many people with a tiny, seemingly insignificant amount of food.

The spiritual meaning is that it wasn't about food at all. It was all about feeding the multitudes - with the word of God. And the disciple's pivotal role in that. Jesus didn't come into the world to feed people bread. He declared that he is the 'Bread of Life.' That he is the 'Living Bread' that came down from heaven to give life to the world.

Jesus commissioned his early disciples to go into the world, preach the gospel, and make disciples of men. The preaching of the gospel is the *preaching* of the word of God. More disciples are then made through the *teaching* of the word of God. The disciples didn't go out carrying loaves of bread. They went forth - with the word of God - the Bread of Life.

Furthermore, the 'feeding' of the five thousand is symbolic of Jesus' disciples, continuing to 'teach them many things.' Only now they were doing it as a team, a team under the direction and instruction of Jesus. Only this time, it was them, not Jesus, who were collectively providing the 'bread.' And, spiritually speaking, the 'bread' they each possessed was the teaching they had received directly from Jesus throughout their walk with him. *That* is why Jesus immediately said, 'You feed them.' That is why he asked them, 'How many loaves do you have, go and see'? What he was saying was, look inside of yourselves, consider the resources I have given you. It's now time for you to use those resources - to feed the multitudes...*just as I have been doing!*

That's why they were called disciples. Because a disciple does the work of his master, he does the work that his master trained him to do. A disciple does the same work as his master. And he does it in the same way that his master does it.

Some things that we simply cannot afford to miss here are, firstly, Jesus said to his disciples 'collectively' what have you got, go and see? This represents the diversity of spiritual gifts and talents that the New Testament teaches that God has given the church throughout the body of Christ. Secondly, it is the responsibility of the church to continue to teach the 'many things' of the full counsel of God from the vast riches of the scriptures. This cannot be done by one or two people within our fellowships; neither was it ever intended to be. In the feeding of the five thousand, all twelve disciples were involved in bringing, distributing, and serving the bread. That is a core element part of the 'blueprint' I refer to.

What our traditions have done is to take the intended function of the many and delegated it to the few. The result is that there are too few teachers and too many listeners.

I believe this is a current illustration of what Jesus referred to as "Making the word of God of none effect through your traditions." By that, I mean 'church' and/or 'doctrinal' traditions, detracting from the intended potential of the full effectiveness and impact of the word of God.

For example; our traditions have evolved to the current state of affairs where we think it's normal for believers to be routinely, repeatedly and continuously taught the word of God by the pastor or minister. Pastors, ministers, and bible teachers are (or should be) individuals who possess the spiritual gift of teaching the word of God.

That God-given ability is so they can skillfully open the scriptures so that the rest of the church is helped to learn and understand the word themselves and then teach and minister it to others. Jesus continually opened the meaning of the scriptures to his disciples. He quite literally 'broke bread' with them. The pastor/teacher's role is precisely the same. They break the word into bite-size digestible chunks so that others can more readily learn to understand it and use it. It is no different or any more complicated than being taught any specialist subject at college or university. The teachers and lecturers are knowledgeable and skilled in their subject, and they facilitate learning in their students. No college on earth has students being taught the same subject week in, week out, year after year but who never graduate in order to work in their respective fields.

It stands to reason that the fewer teachers (disciples) there are in the field, the fewer among the multitudes will be impacted. Jesus declared then, and it resonates even louder today "The fields are white unto harvest, but the labourers are few." To put it another way: The multitudes need to know about the good news, but there are not enough people telling them. Or; Society needs direction, but there are not enough Christians teaching them.

I am presenting the feeding of the five thousand as a 'masterclass' in how the church is supposed to work. Whilst Jesus is the 'Master' of the church in every sense of the term, in the feeding of the five thousand, he modeled the role of a pastor, and his disciples naturally played the part of the disciples. But more specifically - the church. (The church, after all, is simply - Christ's disciples working together - as a team) The church as it began then, and the church as it should still function now today. Like a pastor today, Jesus did the main teaching. But it was the disciples who then did the work - based upon his teaching. It was the disciples who gathered the 'food.' It was the disciples who organised and managed the crowd of people. And it was the disciples who served the 'bread' to the multitudes. So, Jesus - the teacher, modeled to his disciples how they also should be teachers.

Ephesians 4:11-13 says that Christ gave certain 'ministry gifts' to the church. He made certain people to be apostles, prophets, evangelists and pastors, and teachers. The term pastors and teachers are best understood as a joint ability of pastor/teacher. Essentially someone who is gifted in both nurturing and teaching people. It goes on to explain what their job involves and is as follows:

- *'To equip the saints'*

- *To ensure the Christian has the knowledge and skills they need to do the work of a disciple of Christ. A fundamental and crucial part of which is to ensure that the Christian knows how to feed themselves the word - in order to be able to feed others also. What with? With the word!*

- *For the work of the ministry.'*

- *So that the Christian can witness and teach others. Namely, to go into all the (their) world - proclaiming the good news and making (other) disciples. Who will also in time - teach the word.*

- *'For the building up and encouragement of the body of Christ'*

- *So that the Christian (every Christian) can also encourage, teach, and support others.*

So we see that it is *not* the pastor/minister's job to do all the ministry in order to perpetually encourage the congregation.

It is no different from studying any subject at college or university for the purpose of pursuing a career in that subject. The lecturer/tutor introduces and breaks down the subject matter under various categories and sections in order to help the student learn it for themselves, just like the pastor/teacher at church. In due course, the student goes out into the world, 'equipped' to do the job. Very oddly when it comes to church, many Christians never 'leave college' That, I believe, is precisely the reason that "the labourers (in the specialist career of being a disciple of Jesus) are few."

I believe we have inadvertently 'warehoused' a mighty army of disciples by containing them within a culture and a tradition of 'attending meetings.'

But herein is another fundamental problem. A fundamental Christian problem, which I believe lies at the very core of certain issues facing the church today. Issues such as believers moving from church to church, or dipping in and out of fellowship, and many believers failing to attend a place of worship regularly, or not at all.

This particular problem is, I believe, rooted in the misconception that church life exists to predominantly meet the needs of the Christian, rather than it being focused on training and developing Christians to serve and to meet the needs of others.

This state of affairs, this "tradition of men" has evolved and has become an illusion or, a false picture, of what church is and it has resulted in a culture whereby many Christians today simply do not adequately study the bible for themselves with a view to sharing their knowledge with those around them. If a Christian is not habitually reading/using the bible as their daily food, they quite simply will not understand their place and role within church or the function of the body of Christ. Neither will they be able to adequately teach others.

Being a disciple of Jesus should first and foremost mean to be a disciple of his word. That is the stock-in-trade of a disciple. That is what we carry. That is our product. That is our message. The word is the 'business' we are in.

Remember the 'Lord's Prayer' - we are instructed to pray (ask) that God will "give us this day our daily bread." That daily bread is not referring to natural food; it is referring to the word of God. Lord give us our daily intake of the word of God. That is the bible, the scriptures. Every day the disciple of Jesus should be taking in the scriptures with the same approach as taking in natural food. And that spiritual food - the word of God, once we have developed a 'taste' for it, becomes a daily pleasure. Something that we don't want to do without any more that we would want to miss meals.

Just to expand on this point. Jesus specifically taught his disciples *not* to ask God for daily food. "Seek not therefore what you shall eat, what you shall drink and how you shall be clothed, but seek first the kingdom of God and his righteousness and all of these things will be added (given) to you because your Heavenly Father already knows that you have need of these things." In other words, he told us not to ask/pray for those things. Why? Because there is no need. God already knows, and God already provides. Think about it this way: Our children don't have to ask us to feed them. Of course they don't, it's our responsibility because they are ours and we love them. It would sound ridiculous if when my children were small, they said: "Daddy, please feed me today." We do however expect our children to 'learn' and to apply themselves to learning. Increasingly so, the older they get. It's precisely the same with our Heavenly Father. He will take care of us, but he expects *us* to learn and grow and develop and mature.

Taking care of us is his responsibility. Growing into maturity is ours.

Furthermore, when we look at what is commonly known as 'The Lord's Prayer,' everything that Jesus teaches us to pray for relates to our spiritual life, not our physical life. To the spiritual dimension of our lives, not the physical.

Let's look at it: (words in brackets mine)

Our Father in heaven.

Hallowed (Holy) be your name.

Your kingdom come. Your will be done on earth (in and through my life) as it is in heaven.

Give us this day our daily bread.(meaning our daily 'spiritual' bread).

And forgive us our debts, as we forgive our debtors.

(Other translations use the term 'trespasses' or 'offences' for 'debts' and 'debtors'. It essentially means to ask God to forgive us our sins, offences or misdeeds - as we forgive anyone who commits sins, offences or misdeeds against us)

And do not lead us unto temptation (or, do not allow us to be led into temptation) but deliver us from the evil one. For yours is the kingdom and the power and the glory forever, amen. (Matthew 6:9-13)

So we see, everything Jesus instructs us to pray for, that is, everything he instructs us to ask for, to want, to desire from God - is spiritual. And that crucially includes: Give me (please supply to me) today (and every day) with my daily bread. Which means my daily 'spiritual' bread. The word of God, the Bible, the scriptures, *is* that bread. And the only way to get words into our 'being' is to read them.

However - God simply cannot give us our daily bread - if we fail to 'eat.'

We also notice in the Lord's Prayer that daily bread is the very first thing we are instructed to ask for. The correlation here is very clear. We need food every single day for us to be physically healthy fit, and strong. Our bodies are thereby able to grow, mature, and flourish as well as resist and fight illness. So, daily physical food is a fundamental part of our very existence. It is the first and foremost part of everyday life. Without it, we would very quickly become weak and faint and susceptible to illness. I believe that it is the same in the spiritual dimension of our lives. We simply cannot expect to be spiritually strong and healthy, creative and energetic, etc., if we don't 'eat' spiritual food.

Jesus declared, "Man (people) cannot live by bread alone, but by every word that proceeds from the mouth of God shall man live." But wait a minute, very many people, those who don't have Christ in their lives, 'do' live. So, people can live by bread (natural food) alone. True, but they are not alive spiritually. The bible teaches that without Christ in our lives, we are all "dead in trespasses and sins." That is precisely why the Bible also says to the Christian, "You has he quickened (made alive) who *were* dead in trespasses and sins."

Before a person, any and every person, accepts Christ as Saviour, they are spiritually dead. They are dead to God. Dead to the knowledge of God. And dead to any relationship with God. They are spiritually dead, even though they are physically alive.

So when Jesus said, "Man cannot live by bread alone," he was referring to 'fully living.' That is, being alive both physically and spiritually. To be only physically alive, you only need to be sustained with physical/natural food. But to also be spiritually alive, a person needs both natural and spiritual food to sustain them and keep them strong and healthy, both physically and spiritually.

Is it possible to be both physically and spiritually alive (which is precisely what a Christian is) but be spiritually weak and sickly? Absolutely!

How does that happen? Simple, it happens when a Christian, any Christian, does not feed on the word of God.

They are spiritually alive through the grace of God, but they are not spiritually healthy, strong, resilient, productive, and fruitful. They simply can't be—no more than anyone could be physically or naturally healthy who doesn't eat food regularly or properly.

This links us to yet another problem. Another 'tradition of men.' And it's this: Babies need to be weaned. That is, they need to be encouraged not to rely on milk, so they are gradually introduced to solid food. They need to develop a taste for it. Then and only then do they learn to feed themselves - but feed themselves they must. Their mother nurtures them and teaches them how to do that, and they go on to feed themselves from a relatively young age and for the rest of their lives. In due course, they learn to feed others as well, and so the cycle of life continues.

Just try to imagine for a moment, a society where babies never came off milk and never learned to feed themselves.

I'm sure you know the scripture; "As newborn babes desire the sincere milk of the word that you may grow thereby." But 'milk' is for babies - not for adults.

Yet our churches are filled with Christians who have little or no idea how to feed themselves. Their intake of the word of God is little more than what they hear from the platform on Sunday and maybe a twenty-minute read at some point during the week from a Christian devotional publication such as UCB or similar. And maybe, just maybe, cross-referenced with the actual Bible itself. This is often referred to as having a 'quiet time' with the Lord. I believe that many Christians hold the view that if they have that daily quiet time, that twenty minutes each day in Bible reading and prayer, that they have met some sort of acceptable spiritual criteria.

I believe that this is largely because real discipleship is not taught to the extent that it should be. Instead, Christians are often 'fed' the milk of the word over and over again, but not taught or encouraged to become disciplined readers of the bible for themselves. It is not my intention to sound critical or negative—quite the opposite.

I'm simply trying to point out something profoundly fundamental and core to the Christian life and the life of the church. Something so simple, so wonderful, so beautiful and so powerful, but something that we have missed and buried to some extent under 'our church traditions' and it's this:

That absolutely every believer is called to be a disciple of Jesus. And that, first and foremost, should mean to be a disciple of his word.

To be a disciple means to follow closely, to adhere to, to learn from, and to be taught by someone. The Oxford dictionary definition is; A person who is a pupil or an adherent of the doctrines of another. That spells out one thing: Dedication. Dedication to learning what Jesus taught. Dedication to understanding what his teaching means. And dedication to learning how it applies to each one of us individually. *And* what it requires us to do.

Jesus taught: "If you continue in my word, *then* you will truly be my disciples.

Remember, Jesus personally and intimately took his disciples aside regularly and expounded the meaning of the scriptures to them. The scriptures were Jesus' language. He taught his disciples that language. Christians today should be able to speak that language. Yet so very many believers are impoverished when it comes to their knowledge, understanding, and articulation of the word of God. Yet, if they did read it every day, that would simply not be the case.

Are we guilty of somehow having moved significantly away from what Jesus himself required of a disciple to where we are today, namely a Sunday sermon, a bible study group once a week, and a brief 'quiet time' each day?

Consider this scenario: We visit a restaurant on a Sunday and have a hearty meal. A Sunday dinner prepared and served to us by someone else. We didn't have to do anything other than turn up, eat the meal, pay for it then leave. But then from Monday to Saturday we just live on snacks. Maybe a ten-minute snack in the morning. Or a ten-minute snack before we go to bed. Then on Sunday, back to the restaurant to sit down and be served again with a decent meal. Sounds ridiculous, doesn't it? Yet, for many Christians, that is precisely their approach to the word of God. They simply don't appear to see or feel the need to spend time preparing and eating their own 'food' at home during the week.

Tragically this 'Sunday restaurant scenario' pretty much sums up the approach to the word of God of many believers today.

Getting back to the text: Jesus said to his disciples, "How many loaves do you have, go and see?"

What he was in essence saying was: You already have the resources amongst yourselves to meet this need, you just don't know it yet - because you just don't understand how this all works yet.

The disciples then enquired among themselves to find out what resources they could 'collectively' draw from to meet the needs presented before them. That is precisely how the church, the body of Christ, is still supposed to function today. And that is how, if understood, adhered to and applied, both the individual Christian and the church could function considerably more abundantly and dynamically today.

We are considering the event of the feeding of the five thousand to be the blueprint of how the church is designed to function. The principles we see enacted with Jesus, and his disciples would later be taught throughout the epistles (letters) in the New Testament. That's what I mean when I say that if we can grasp those principles that are outworked in this 'masterclass,' the pages of the New Testament will become clearer to us. For example, in Jesus asking his disciples "How many loaves do you have, or, in other words "what have you got?" - we see New Testament teaching about what Christians do in fact inherently possess. Let's look at First Corinthians Chapter 12. Here are extracts from that chapter: (words in brackets added)

- *There are diversities of gifts, but the same Spirit*
- *There are differences of ministries, but the same Lord*

- *And there are diversities of activities, but the same God who works all in all (in and through you all)*

- *But the manifestation of the Spirit is given to each one (each person) for the profit of all (other people)*

- *For to one is given the word of wisdom through the Spirit*

- *To another the word of knowledge through the same Spirit*

- *To another faith by the same Spirit*

- *To another gifts of healing by the same Spirit*

- *To another the working of miracles*

- *To another prophecy*

- *To another discerning of spirits*

- *To another different kinds of tongues*

- *To another the interpretation of tongues*

- *But one and the same Spirit works all these things, distributing to each one (each person) individually as He wills (or, according to the will of God)*

- *For as the (human) body is one (one body) and has many members (many parts) but all the members (parts) of that one body, being many (parts) so also is (the spiritual body of) Christ.*

- *For in fact the body (the body of Christ/the church) is not one member but many*

- *But now God has set the members, each one of them, in the body just as He pleased*

- *But (so) now there are many (different) members, yet one body*

- *Now you are (each) members of the body of Christ, and members individually*

This main theme and substance of 1st Corinthians, Chapter 12, can also be found in Romans, Chapter 12 and Ephesians, Chapter 4

[4]There is one body and one Spirit even as you are called in one hope of your calling [5]One God and Father of (you) all, who is above (you)

6all and through (you) all, and in you all 7But unto every one of us is given grace according to the measure of the gift of Christ. (Ephesians 4:4-7)

This chapter of 'Apples of Gold' is not about studying the gifts of the spirit in detail. I merely take the reader to these scriptures in order to give an example of just some of the principles demonstrated in the feeding of the five thousand from a wider scriptural perspective.

There is a current particular 'doctrinal' view that the gifts of the spirit, as taught in scripture, are no longer for today. That viewpoint, in my opinion, is a very unfortunate and specific 'tradition of men.' One that has tragically closed the minds of many Christians and significantly restricted their comprehension of the kingdom of God and of the centrality of the Holy Spirit in the effective functioning of the church.

It is the gifts of the Holy Spirit that equip the individual Christian for their role in the kingdom. The 'gifts' of the Spirit are the characteristics, abilities, and 'talents' of Christ himself. The very talents that he manifested throughout his ministry on earth. In the book of Ephesians, it specifically and clearly explains that when Jesus ascended to heaven, he gave these gifts to the church. And that he gives a different gift or gifts to different people, through the Holy Spirit and in accordance with his will, plans, and purposes. Only some of those 'diverse' gifts are listed above. I would draw to your attention that these spiritual gifts have been given to *every* believer. Also, in Ephesians 4:16, we are taught that the whole body (the church):

- Is properly joined together
- And held together
- By that which every part supplies
- According to (or depending on) the effective working
- Of every (each) part
- So the body grows and increases
- And builds itself up

Finally, in the same chapter, v 12 teaches that all these gifts are given to the church *For the equipping of the saints (the believer) for the work of the ministry.*

Therefore, God has given every believer - spiritual gifts as a means of equipping them, every one of them - for the work of the ministry.

Section 5- The Plan Put Into Action

So let's now fast-forward from all those years ago, to that scene in Judea where Jesus was holding a masterclass with his disciples, demonstrating to them how the church can meet the needs of the multitudes - to now with us, his disciples in the 21st century. Let's revisit that scene and compare it to today - here and now. I'm sure we all agree that around us in society today, there are 'multitudes' in need. I am specifically referring to spiritual needs.

As Christians, our heart's desire is for God, our Heavenly Father, to meet those needs.

In other words, we deeply desire they will come to the knowledge of God through the Lord Jesus and be saved. The task of reaching them, for many reasons, seems overwhelming. We try to share our faith with those who will listen, but it somehow often doesn't seem enough. We invite people to come to church, but that also doesn't seem enough. We pray earnestly for family members, neighbours, work colleagues, etc., yet the multitudes don't seem to be reached. If you are like me, you'll know what it's like to say - Lord, what can I do? And as part of our home churches and fellowship's, Lord, what can we do? The need is too great. How can they all be fed (reached)? And on our hearts we cry - Lord (you) do something.

That is almost like saying - send them away. It's perhaps an unconscious way of detaching or distancing ourselves from the problem. We feel that the solution to such great need surely must lie somewhere else.

Jesus would say to us today, or to put it another way - He still says to us today - "You feed them." You meet the need. And we would answer - How can we possibly do that? And he would reply - "What have you got - go and see?" Or to put it another way....' just think about it.'

You see, what Jesus was saying to his disciples then - and what, I believe, he is still saying to his disciples today, is this: *You* have the answer. *You* have the resources. *You* possess the means to meet the need. Not just individually but especially collectively. (I will speak more about the 'collective' aspect shortly) And we may ask - but how can that be? The answer is this; As Christians:

- We each have a relationship with God through Christ.
- We each have the life of Christ living within us.
- We each have some aspects of the gifts of the spirit.
- We each have the testimony of how we found Christ (the testimony of our salvation)
- We each have testimonies of experiences of God's goodness, breakthroughs, deliverances, provision, healing, etc.
- We each possess divine (supernatural) peace, love, joy, hope, faith, eternal assurance, etc.
- We each carry the word of God - which is the very means of salvation to anyone and everyone.
- We each have the capacity to possess more of the incredible riches contained within the scriptures, which is the living word of God and able to meet any need.
- We are each priests in the household of God and are thereby able to intercede in prayer on behalf of others.

So when Jesus asks us "what have you got?" - what should our answer be?

But herein is yet another fundamental problem. At the feeding of the five thousand, Jesus' disciples didn't think they had much, if anything, to offer. This is exemplified in their statement: We have five loaves and two fish. To put that another way, they said: *we only have* five loaves and two fish. Implicit within their statement surely must have been the thought - what use is that going to be? Five thousand hungry people and between us, *we only have!*

Is it not the same today? So much need, such enormous challenges, but like the early disciples, we often think - we only have. I truly believe that the church and the individual Christian today is facing precisely the same dilemma that the disciples faced then. I also believe that as the disciples then were about to receive life-changing revelation about just how God 'works' - that we too can also receive the very same revelation today. The things that happened next are truly remarkable. I will outline them under the heading of three New Testament Church Principles.

Principle 1 - The Principle of Giving

Upon the disciples producing the loaves and the fish, Jesus didn't further discuss things with them. He didn't explain what he was about to do. He never even mentioned the loaves and the fish. Why? Because (in this kingdom masterclass), the first 'church principle' had been established.

What was that principle? It was this; they simply brought to him what they had. He was going to do the rest. There is something here that we simply must firmly grasp if we are to better understand the 'miraculous' aspect of church and how it is designed to operate - and it's this: Jesus could have fed all those people himself in an instant with a single word. But, *he has chosen to work through his church.* That was the case then, and it is still the case now. If we fail to see and understand that plan (that blueprint) and to fall in line with it - all other approaches, ideas, or programmes, no matter how well-intended, simply cannot succeed. That *is* his plan. His plan is to work with the church. His plan is to work through the church. And each and every Christian *in* the church. The scriptures provide us with no Plan B - and we shouldn't attempt to create one!

The disciples had simply brought what they had - to him. And that was enough. *That* was all they were required to do. That was all they were required to do then - and that is all we are required to do now. They 'collectively' brought what 'little' substance they had - as a contribution to the great needs of the multitude.

When we say to God 'I only have' - his answer is, I only want what you 'only' have.

That sounds just too simple to be true, doesn't it? That sounds just too simple to possibly make any real difference. However - therein that simplicity is a significant shift from the prevailing approach to church life today. The disciple's simple response, as instructed and directed by Jesus, to meet the needs of the multitude was to bring the 'little that they had' and giving it to him. He then did the rest!

Many Christians today 'go to church' - to receive. However, our true calling is to 'be the church' - and to give.

Principle 2 - The Principle of Structure and Fellowship

Jesus then "commanded" his disciples to make all the people sit down by companies on the green grass. And they sat down in ranks of hundreds and fifties.

His language here is noticeably very assertive and directive - as opposed to being passive and his instructions optional. Principle 2 is the principle of structure, order, and community in the church. Jesus *commanded* this model of structure, namely, that the people should be in companies. That means fellowship. That means that every Christian should be part of a fellowship, part of the local church. To sit on the green grass speaks of being at ease and rest in a place of pastoral care and nurture. Far too many believers today have unwittingly adopted society's philosophy of individualism. They either pick and choose or chop and change which church they attend. Or they decide not to commit to a company of believers at all. Then they wonder why the church isn't working out for them or why the church isn't as effective and powerful as it should be. They completely fail to realise that it is precisely because they aren't bringing what they have, that the church doesn't have all the resources God intends it to have. Resources that are designed to equip, enrich, and empower the individual Christian and the collective church so they can both be all that they should be.

Believers who withhold their gifts, talents, and service in this way are failing to function and serve in their calling as disciples of Jesus.

A very significant point within the details of the account of the feeding of the five thousand is this: Jesus told his disciples to 'find out (learn/understand) what they had' and bring it - *to him*. What does that mean? It means that as his disciples, we are each meant to "seek first the kingdom." That includes seeking to discover and understand what our particular spiritual gifts and talents are.

And also, where and how God wants us to serve the local church with 'what we have.'

It's the Lord Jesus who we each serve. It's him we bring our gifts to. It's him we submit our lives to. It's him who we serve.

We don't connect with the Lord through the church - we connect with the church through our personal relationship with the Lord. However, we serve him - together, in and through the church.

Principle 3 - The Principle of Divine Multiplication

Jesus then took the five loaves and the two fish, and he did four things:

1. He looked up to heaven

2. He blessed it

3. He broke the bread

4. He gave the bread and the fish to his disciples to distribute to the people

In looking up to heaven, Jesus connected with the heavenly spiritual realm, with his Father, where there are no limitations, no lack, and where nothing is impossible. In blessing the bread and the fish, he was approving and establishing the kingdom principles that were being outworked. He was sealing the fact that this was how he would work in partnership with his church - as Head of the Church - then and forever.

In breaking the bread and dividing the fish, he, as only he alone can, hugely multiplied that which his disciples had brought to him. In giving the bread and the fish back to his disciples (in miraculously multiplied volume), Jesus demonstrated that it is to be his disciples who are to serve the multitudes with 'spiritual' food. Spiritual food is the "bread of life." And the bread of life, as we know, is the word of God.

It then goes on to say that the five thousand people all ate to the full. And that after they had all eaten, they took up twelve *full* baskets containing the fragments (what was leftover) from the bread and the fish. There is simply only one word that can describe how five loaves of bread and two fish can feed five thousand people, with surplus baskets of food leftover, and that word is - Miraculous! There is simply no denying it and no rationalising it. It was by far much too abundant and extravagant and involving such huge numbers of people, to be anything other than an amazing miracle. An amazing display of God's limitless power, his limitless capacity, and his limitless ability to provide. This miracle cannot be explained in human terms, and it cannot be understood by natural means. It didn't occur of itself. It didn't just happen.

Furthermore, it didn't happen for no reason. This miracle was the result of a process. And that process served to demonstrate a purpose. That purpose was that Jesus was demonstrating to his disciples, then - and to his disciples now - principles upon which the church is designed to function.

As Christians today, we may ask - Lord, where are the miracles? The Lord might reply - where are the principles?

The principles that I showed you in the beginning. The principles I demonstrated amongst my first disciples. He might add - I have not changed. Those principles have not changed. I have not changed them. It's you who has changed. If you want to see the same results as at the feeding of the five thousand - understand and apply those principles.

Footnote:

I'd like to briefly clarify my understanding of two of the elements of this chapter.

1. That every believer and disciple of Jesus should be a disciple of his word.

I don't mean that every Christian should be an expert in their knowledge of the entire bible. I don't mean we are all meant to be theologians. And I don't mean we all have to be able to quote reams of scripture and verse fluently.

I do believe that the Christian should, in time, become very familiar with all that Jesus taught. As such they should become gradually and increasingly knowledgeable about the gospels. They should particularly become conversant with the parables that Jesus used, including their spiritual meaning *and* their application. They are, after all, the 'language' of the kingdom. The language that Jesus himself used. It stands to reason that the disciple of Jesus should aspire to understand, apply, and also model and teach to others, the very same things that Jesus did. I also believe that all Christians should become increasingly familiar with the epistles (letters) in the New Testament. I see it this way; it was the truth within the gospels that brought us to Christ - and it is the epistles that essentially explain what happened to us when we were 'converted.' They also deal with the many threads and themes of spiritual life, including our relationship with God, our relationship with other believers, and our role and function within the church.

Furthermore, when Christians don't personally apply themselves to developing an understanding of the bible, they cannot truly benefit from teaching and preaching within the church. Therein is a 'double problem.' Firstly, they cannot truly benefit from teaching, which could help, support, instruct and mature them. Why? - because they don't understand biblical or spiritual 'language.'

Secondly, the pastor or teacher's task is made more difficult, less effective, or even ineffective, precisely because of this. This is exactly the kind of scenario I have referred to earlier. One that can become a fixed and long term (fruitless) pattern.

2. That every believer and disciple of Jesus should be a teacher of the word.

I don't mean that every believer is supposed to be a teacher in the sense of being academically or theologically qualified, specially trained, or spiritually gifted as a bible teacher. God has indeed placed all such offices within the wider church for them to fulfill their specific roles.

What I do mean is that every believer should strive to obtain at least a good basic understanding of their faith. And what they need to do that is predominantly contained within scripture. It really is no different to us, each developing an understanding of our natural lives, the world around us and our place, purpose, and role within it. We attend primary school, then secondary school, and perhaps go on to further education. In any event - *we learn*.

Furthermore, we are continually learning. Slowly but surely, gradually and incrementally and by age and stage appropriate measures. We learn what we need to learn each step of the way. And what we each learn is sufficient for the stage we are at. This 'natural growth' continually demands our personal application to study related materials if we are to properly grow and mature. Then over time, what we have learned becomes almost second nature. We don't however do this by ourselves or within a social vacuum.

We have teachers, mentors, subject materials, study groups, books, friends and family, etc. In due course, we each achieve a basic education. One which we can then build upon, depending upon and according to our line of work and our role within society. We are then, at the very least, conversant with the subject/s at hand. We are thereby gradually each becoming 'teachers' inasmuch as we have developed knowledge and understanding that we can pass on to others. If we transfer this 'natural life' process to our spiritual lives and our function within the church and the wider community - but our subject of study is Jesus and all that he stands for and represents; *that* is what I understand it means that every believer should be a teacher! From a biblical perspective; A disciple of Jesus' teaching who is sufficiently knowledgeable and experienced to be able to teach and *disciple* others.

Chapter Five

The Four Friends

(*Teamwork, innovation & breakthrough*)

Gospel of Mark. Chapter 2: 1-12

[1]And again He entered Capernaum after some days, and it was heard that He was in the house. [2]Immediately many gathered together, so that there was no longer room to receive them, not even near the door. And He preached the word to them. [3]Then they came to Him, bringing a paralytic who was carried by four men. [4]And when they could not come near Him because of the crowd, they uncovered the roof where He was. So when they had broken through, they let down the bed on which the paralytic was lying.

[5]When Jesus saw their faith, He said to the paralytic, "Son, your sins are forgiven you." [6]And some of the scribes were sitting there and reasoning in their hearts, [7]"Why does this Man speak blasphemies like this? Who can forgive sins but God alone?"

[8]But immediately, when Jesus perceived in His spirit that they reasoned thus within themselves, He said to them, "Why do you reason about these things in your hearts? [9]Which is easier, to say to the paralytic, 'Your sins are forgiven you,' or to say, 'Arise, take up your bed and walk'? [10]But that you may know that the Son of Man has power on earth to forgive sins"—He said to the paralytic, [11]"I say to you, arise, take up your bed, and go to your house." [12]Immediately he arose, took up the bed, and went out in the presence of them all, so

that all were amazed and glorified God, saying, "We never saw anything like this!"

This is one of the first scriptural 'pictures' I saw as a young Christian. Like the others in this book, it struck me with its brevity and simplicity whilst at the same time containing so much biblical truth along particular themes. In this case, one of those themes is around unorthodox evangelism. Not that I suppose, scripturally speaking, there is such a thing as orthodox evangelism in the first place. But I think it's fair to say that there are perceived 'traditional' church approaches which have become something of the norm.

Another theme is teamwork. For me, teamwork is encapsulated in the New Testament doctrine of "body ministry," or to put it another way, the ministry of the body of Christ. It has been said; If it isn't teamwork, it won't work. And from a doctrinal and ministry perspective, that is a view I personally fully endorse. Yet, so very often, we see believers not engaging in teamwork at all. Worse, of course, is them not engaging in any kind of Christian service whatsoever.

The third theme is innovation and breakthrough. Or, innovation that leads to breakthrough. Put together; I think these themes add up to what might be called radical Christianity. There are two inferences within this context to the word radical. Radical is an extract from the Latin word radix, which means 'root.' So, radical refers to that which is original or close to the source. If something is grown from its original root, then it will have the form it was intended to have. So we see within this story, radical actions taken by a group of friends in their efforts to get an incapacitated man to meet Jesus. In this respect it is radical because that's the way it should be done. It's true to form. It's true to its roots.

We discover that when they had tried and failed to get their friend to see Jesus by conventional methods, namely through the front door of the house he was in, rather than give up, they took radical measures to get the job done. But this was radical in the other sense of the word. We are most familiar with radical meaning, something being outwith the conventional and normal. In this respect, their actions were radical because their conduct became increasingly unconventional, socially questionable, controversial, and even included them inflicting damage to the property that Jesus was in at the time. Yet, as we shall see, Jesus evidently saw nothing untoward in their actions; on the contrary, he approved of it and even commended their efforts.

So, let's look at the picture presented to us. Jesus was visiting a certain town, and the news was out that he was in someone's house. A big crowd had gathered, the house was now full, and a large crowd of people was outside trying to get inside or at least somehow get close enough to see and hear what was going on. Entering this scene are four people; let's assume for convenience that they were men, and let's also assume they were all friends. These four men were carrying another man on what is described as a bed because he was sick. So, the man was sick to the extent that he couldn't walk in order to get himself to Jesus and needed to be carried lying on a bed of sorts by four other people. I think it is quite alright to assume that as any kind of bed has four corners and that as four of his friends were carrying him, that they each had a corner of the bed to hold onto. Let us further assume that this bed was a modified stretcher with some sort of handles attached. So, we have an incapacitated man being carried on a stretcher by four friends, each holding one handle of the stretcher.

The first startling thing for me in this picture is that this man didn't have the capacity to get himself to Jesus. He had to be carried there. Furthermore, it required several people to carry him. Each one was carrying their share of the load, their share of the burden. Each one was holding up his own corner. Two men could have carried their friend, but it would have meant twice the burden, twice the weight, and it would have proved twice as difficult. And it would have taken twice as long to accomplish. One man could conceivably have carried the load alone, but that would have proved extremely difficult. However, the burden did not fall to one man, or two men, no, the pattern, and the plan was a shared weight, an equal burden, a manageable, achievable, shared task. Each man having to use only one hand to carry the needs of another whilst his other hand was free.

That speaks to me of balance, life balance, church balance, ministry balance, and overall spiritual balance.

The fact is that only one man or two men simply could not have been so innovative, creative, and persistent in their mission. It required teamwork, shared responsibility, cooperation, and coordination to get the job done. Think about it for a minute. Four men carrying another man on a stretcher, just walking in a straight line and with no obstacles in the way, in itself requires teamwork involving very fine coordination and balance. Let's put it this way; they would have to be stepping in time, marching to the same tune, so to speak—what a great picture of how the church is meant to function. Every person was carrying their corner of responsibility, not too little and not too much. Moving forward together, fulfilling the great commission, which, as we all know, is to bring others to Christ. Each person knew their place. Yet, tragically this is all too often just not the case. Rather, we see some struggling under too much weight and others carrying very little weight or none at all.

That this man was incapacitated and unable to get himself to Jesus is very significant. The truth is, none of us who are now Christians knew how to get to Jesus. We were incapacitated by the blindness of ignorance and sin. It took someone to make an effort to tell us about Christ and the gospel. They took the time and made an effort to 'carry' us to the good news. To point us to where we could find God through an encounter with Christ. In fact, for many of us, it was more than one person who led us towards Christ. Perhaps a work colleague, a friend, or a family member was the very first person to share their testimony with us. Then we heard more about Christ from someone else. Or we attended church or a Christian event and heard the gospel preached. The preacher 'carried' that message to us. Then, once we had accepted Jesus, we will have met other believers who, one way or another, would have extended friendship, fellowship, and support to us. In that way, we were, in fact, 'carried' by others to an encounter with Jesus and then further carried into kingdom life and towards spiritual growth and service.

I believe this to be the case concerning everyone who does not yet know Christ. Like us before them, they simply don't know how to get there. Like the man on the stretcher, they are incapacitated, but in a spiritual sense. They are incapacitated by the blindness of their heart, by the influence and power of sin. And by the influence and power of the world. Influences and powers that are innately opposed to God. Those without Christ don't even know they need him, let alone how to find him. What am I saying? I'm saying that we must never assume that our unsaved neighbours, colleagues, friends, and loved ones will somehow one day decide they need God, then walk through the front door of the nearest church and get saved. It's not so much as they don't know how to, they don't even know they need to. And even when they are told by Christians that they need to, they generally, initially don't want to. They are incapacitated quite literally from the very start.

In my case, the first I heard anything about Christ was from a very brief conversation with a work colleague when I was still in my teens and living in the Channel Islands. I remember that what he said sounded odd but interesting. I certainly didn't think it had any impact on me at the time, and as far as I was concerned, I promptly put it out of my mind and went to the pub. A later encounter when I was living in London, was with a 'religious' couple who were going from door to door on a Sunday. I talked to them a couple of times and thought that they at least appeared to have some depth to them. But what they had to say about God didn't register with me. A few years later, after moving to Scotland, it was a relative, my sister-in-law Heather, who began telling me about Jesus. She told me she had recently been 'saved,' and whilst I had no idea what that meant, I could definitely see she had something that I didn't.

Around that time, I was sensing very deeply; there was something wrong with my life, something missing. I saw in my sister-in-law that she had that something special though I didn't understand it at all. She seemed to have peace and contentment. There was even a tangible aura around her.

But like the incapacitated man on the stretcher, I could do nothing to help myself. Why am I telling you my story? I'm telling you because though I was totally oblivious to it at the time - I realised much later that I was being 'carried.' Like the man on the stretcher, God was placing his people around me. Over the space of several years, whether I was in the Channel Islands, London, or Scotland, each person was taking a corner of the stretcher I was lying on. Each one carrying their share of the burden. Each slowly but surely carrying me towards Jesus. Not long after my first conversations with Heather, I met another Christian.

My wife and I were in the process of buying a flat, and he was the mortgage broker. He visited one Saturday afternoon, and after settling the mortgage details, he then began to talk, without any prompting from me, about how God had changed his life. Once again, I didn't understand much of what he said, and he said a lot, but what did strike me was that whilst he was a completely different kind of character to my sister-in-law, he seemed to have the very same sense of presence or aura around him. And it was predominantly one of confidence, calm and peace. After spending a long time talking to us, he invited us to attend a church service with him the following day. To be perfectly honest, it was just to get rid of him that I reluctantly agreed to his invitation. Church was not, neither ever had been part of my worldview. He said he would pick us up at 5.30 pm the next day. I had no intention of going with him. You see, I was being carried. I knew I was 'sick.' I knew that better than anyone. I knew I needed help, but I had no intention of seeking it. I knew there was something wrong with my life, but I didn't have a clue what it was or how to fix it. But God knew, and all along, he had been mobilizing a variety of his people to carry me to the source of my cure. To carry me to the Great Physician.

The point I'm making is this: each of those unconnected and unrelated Christians was doing their job simply by telling me about Jesus. Simply by taking the time and making an effort to reach out to me out of concern and compassion. They were taking a risk. I wasn't always too friendly, agreeable, or even sober. My background was pubs and drugs, and I was very obviously not 'church' material. Yet by each of them being at their station, by each taking a corner of my bed, by each going a short distance with me as God directed them, they collectively got me "to the house where Jesus was." The incredible thing is that they each had no idea that their individual efforts and work of ministry was being coordinated by the Holy Spirit to get me where I needed to be. My case is just like millions of others who find Jesus. God uses his church, his saints, his people, to reach out and to "carry" the lost to himself.

When we obediently take our corner and carry our share of the load, we are fulfilling the great commission. The outcomes and the end results are in God's hands. Only he knows the plans he has for a person's life. Our very privileged role is to simply be there and be willing to play our part. When you and I witness to someone, we may, at times, think it was insignificant or ineffective. How wrong we can be. The truth is we have absolutely no idea who God has already used to speak to that person or who he will use next to touch them again in the future.

On the Saturday night of the day of my conversation with the mortgage broker, I attended a silver wedding anniversary celebration. On Sunday, I was in no mood to do anything, or go anywhere so much so that I spent the morning and afternoon in bed, and I intended to stay there! Around 4 pm, my wife reminded me that we had agreed to go to church with the mortgage broker. That was the last thing I wanted to be reminded of and also the very last thing I intended to do.

She persisted, and I relented. At 5.30 as planned, he called at our house, and we accompanied him to church. Finally, just like the incapacitated man on the stretcher, I had arrived at the house where Jesus was. I would never have gotten there by myself. I didn't know how to. I had been carried there and carried there over time by various people, each playing their part, each carrying me that little bit nearer my destination. I had been a reluctant patient, a resistant patient, and as I got nearer my destination, an unwilling patient. But God persisted, his people persisted, and they got me to the house where I would hear what Jesus had to say. Where I would personally feel his presence, and I would hear the declaration of the word of God.

What I was to experience that night completely changed me and changed my life immediately, in an instant and forever. That was over forty years ago.

My own story serves to illustrate the church at work on a sort of global scale. What I mean is that it demonstrates how God has his hand on a person and pursues them wherever they go and whatever they do. Distance, circumstances, time, or any other factors cannot hinder or prevent God's divine will and plan to draw us to himself. And he uses his church, members of his body, to reach out to and minister and bless others in the pursuance of his plans. The one thing I feel I should perhaps emphasise is that I was hungry and thirsty for the meaning of life. I was dissatisfied with the seeming shallowness of everything. I somehow sensed that there just had to be more to life, though I had no idea what that might be. The concept of God never entered my thinking. I was strongly anti-religion, and amongst my group of friends, I would have been the one who would be most intolerant of and offensive towards religious people. I say this because the bible says that they that seek him will find him, that he will pour water on those who are thirsty and blessed are those who hunger and thirst for righteousness because they shall be filled. So, in that respect, I think that God saw that I was searching, and he met me at my point of need. My journey and my subsequent experience of salvation was no more special than any other. I was simply in great need. As Jesus said - it is not those who are well that need a physician but those who are sick.

But let's return to the story. Four men were carrying one man - with the sole purpose of bringing him under the sound of the word of God. What a great illustration of God's purpose for our lives. That purpose is that once we have found the truth that we work together to bring others into the truth. Four handles on the stretcher. A common objective. Equal workload. Shared labour. Mutual support. Friendship, encouragement, and fellowship along the way. What a marvellously clear pattern of how the church is designed to function and operate. I truly believe this clearly serves to demonstrate how the kingdom should advance and how every believer is called to serve - and specifically to serve as part of a team. Sadly, today this is all too often just not the case. I find that too many Christians fail to understand the importance of their role and one way or another withdraw and thereby detach themselves from active, committed church participation and involvement.

Consequently, the work of evangelism and church growth both suffer. Such believers often give a variety of reasons for their actions, such as:

- "I'm disillusioned with church and don't attend any. Often accompanied by - anyway you don't have to go to church to be a Christian."

- "I don't agree with any of the churches and just serve the Lord in my own way."

- "I've previously been hurt in church, and that's why I don't go."

- "I'm still looking for the right church for me."

- "My gifts and/or ministry aren't used, so I don't attend."

- "I'm free to go to any church whenever I feel like it."

Such attitudes or belief systems are very often the root cause for those who carry grievances of having been hurt or offended or not feeling they belong. They unrealistically expect all the advantages that come with the kind of dedicated and faithful commitment that leads to strong bonds and relationships being formed, but without real engagement or commitment on their part. There is also the misconception I referred to earlier when believers think that church is there to meet their needs. When it fails to do so, hurt, offense, or criticism often follow.

There are of course many Christians who don't fall into any of these categories, who are very happy and settled within a fellowship and are being very fulfilled and productive. There are also many who are not and who will identify with one or more of the above. Whichever of these situations a believer finds themselves in, the simple solution and indeed the answer to many unresolved 'church issues' they may have, can be found in this account of the four friends carrying a sick man to see Jesus.

Wherever you are, and whatever your 'church situation' is, if you believe just the basic fundamentals of the New Testament, you will appreciate that whilst you may know the truth, all around you in every walk of life, there are many people who do not. Essentially, all that is required of us as believers concerning that reality is that we try somehow to get the gospel message to them. This invariably will normally, at some point, involve getting them to a place where Christians meet and where the word is preached. We all know a person doesn't have to go to a particular place or attend a church meeting in order to get saved.

Very many people make the decision to accept Christ in many other situations and under very different circumstances, often after hearing the testimony of believers. The principles and the core elements of the account of the four friends carrying a man on a stretcher is that the four friends specifically and strategically worked together with the sole, determined focus of getting the man on the stretcher to a place where he could meet Jesus. Now, in reality, that place could be anywhere. In the case in this story, they didn't take the man to the synagogue or the temple, they took him to someone's house. We perhaps need sometimes to remind ourselves that our spiritual walk and service is not all about 'where to go?' But that it should be focussed on who it is that we serve. And then; what to do - and how to do it? What to do? Is to focus on getting people to Christ. How to do it? According to the biblical model is - teamwork. And the fundamental aspects of teamwork here contain certain crucial elements. Elements that I find are lost to many believers and which they urgently need to rediscover.

Remember, I am presenting this biblical narrative as a picture that tells a story. And I am suggesting that all the 'pictures' I present contain considerable weight of New Testament teaching - in very condensed form. Let's now identify just some of them.

The four friends working together represent the ministry of the body of Christ. We are each given spiritual gifts, but they are given to us to benefit others.

Furthermore, God has placed those gifts in his body, the church, in accordance with his will and purposes. Those gifts are given to every person, for the work of the ministry, and the building up of the body of Christ. We are fellow-labourers together with God. We are to work together with him and work together with each other. Ministry is not taught in scripture as a one-man show, a one-man-band or a solo enterprise. Jesus operated as a member of a team. He sent his disciples out in companies, at least two at a time. There are sound reasons for this—support, counsel, accountability, shared talents, collaborative prayer, and many others.

When we encounter believers who do not engage with the church but insist on going it alone, it is a clear contradiction of the biblical model.

The great commandment given by Jesus to his disciples is that we love one another. Love costs. Love challenges. Love makes constant demands upon us. Love sometimes grates, but love makes us grow. It challenges our selfishness and our biases, and it deals with the old nature. A Christian who insists on going it alone is consciously or unconsciously denying and avoiding those things. No believer can either grow spiritually or really minister effectively in isolation. It is quite simply contrary to God's design. Everything in the New Testament presents and demonstrates the church growing, serving, suffering, enduring, overcoming, worshipping, building, and advancing - together.

That they carried the incapacitated man on a stretcher is a clear demonstration of the essential role and function of the church. By the church, I mean, every member of the church. Each believer. Jesus says we are to go into the highways and the byways and call the sick, the halt, and the lame and 'compel' them to come into God's house. To compel is not passive. It is not benign. It is focussed, confident, urgent, and determined.

Every believer should be on a mission in life to bring others to Christ.

I think that it's very important for us to understand that we are not all natural conversationalists or gifted evangelists. Some people find it much easier than others talk to non-Christians about Christ or invite them to church, whilst others may struggle in that area. But we each have different gifts and talents. And it is by using them that we play our part in the work of evangelism. In order to emphasise this point, take the four men who carried the lame man on the stretcher, maybe it was just one of them, perhaps the one with the most outgoing personality, who initially persuaded the man to go and hear Jesus. But he still needed three others to get the job done. And those three others will have had different abilities. Maybe, simply being willing and available was in itself encouragement for the others. Or perhaps one of them provided the stretcher. That aside, without just their physical presence and willingness to help, the task could not have been accomplished. Yet so many believers completely miss the simplicity of this. Only by *being there*, they are serving, they love others, and they are playing their part in doing the work of evangelism, edifying the saints and building the church. When Christians don't engage with the church or go it alone, they quite simply are not doing what God called them to do. On the subject of spiritual gifts and ministries, let me say this; ability without availability is of little use. Availability is every bit as important and more so than ability. It requires no particular talent to carry the corner of a stretcher, just concern, willingness, and commitment. If you have ministry gifts or other spiritual gifting, but you're not there to help, they are of little real value and of limited use.

That the four men completed their task despite difficulties, discouragement, and obstacles, speaks very loudly of New Testament teaching about patience, love, hope, endurance, commitment, perseverance, overcoming trials, determination, and sticking together in the face of adversity and disappointment. It also resonates with the promise of recognition and reward from Jesus himself for a task well done. Finally, it reinforces the great values, advantages, and strengths of teamwork. Where one person might get weak, weary or discouraged, he has three others on hand to support and encourage him.

Returning once again to the story. It is indeed very brief, with only three of the verses describing the actions of the men carrying the stretcher, and even those verses don't give much detail. They simply say that when the men couldn't get near to Jesus because of the crowd of people that they "uncovered the roof" of the house and when they had "broken it up," they let down (lowered) the bed with the sick man on it. So, we have to fill in the missing details to get a fuller picture to truly appreciate this extraordinary scene. The obvious approach to getting a person on a stretcher into any house would naturally be through the front door or a side or back door if there was one.

Clearly that hadn't been possible as its fair to assume they would have tried. Just trying to get the man on the stretcher through any door, while having to jostle through the crowd would have proved difficult, possibly even attracting criticism and complaints, or even verbal abuse. They could have given up at this point and returned home, maybe to try another day. They could have thought - perhaps it's just not meant to be or that it shouldn't be so difficult. No doubt, we all entertain similar thoughts when we are trying to get someone to Jesus, and there are all sorts of obstacles or delays, or resistance and opposition. I believe this story exists in scripture, at least in part, to help us identify with such issues and to not give up despite them. I would think that having failed to gain access through a door that the roof would not have been the next natural option for those four men. Instead, I see them continuing to awkwardly jostle their way around the outside of the house, again pushing through complaining crowds as they tried to gain access through a window. Then when that obviously also failed, they could have again decided they had done their best and given up. But no, they decided there was still hope, still a possibility, still a chance. They decided amongst themselves - all is not yet lost - let's try the roof! Remember, there are four of them, clumsily manhandling a dead-weight on a makeshift stretcher - through a resistant crowd, who they have already annoyed and who were also vigorously competing to get into the house.

Now try to picture this scene. My understanding is that a standard house in that geographic location at that time would have had a flat roof, made of either tiles or straw and that it probably had a covered hatch on it. There possibly might have been a stone stairway at one side of the house but not necessarily. First, they had to fight through the crowds, awkwardly, and strenuously wrestling the man on the stretcher, up onto the roof. What a struggle. What determination. What resolve. What commitment. What friendship. What teamwork! What a great object lesson of how the church, how each of us, should view evangelism. What innovation. What persistence. What would the end result be? As we shall see, it was quite literally to be - Breakthrough!

Now, finally, they are on the roof of the house. Now what? They hadn't thought about that. Don't we sometimes think that because we are serving God and because our intentions are good in that we are trying to win friends and loved ones to Christ, that things should go smoothly and go well? If we're honest, I'm sure we also sometimes think - If God is in this, if God is for us, if God wants this person to be saved, surely things should go more smoothly, surely things should be easier, surely things should work out better. I think we should take a lesson from this story and perhaps let God shift our thinking. The fact is that as we each labour to get people to Christ that there are often obstacles, sometimes considerable. There are setbacks, and there are challenges. That's just the reality of life. I'm sure, in my case, the various people who were part of my journey to becoming a Christian must have experienced obstacles. Practical obstacles in their own lives as well as the obstacles that I presented. They must have each though at some point - I'll never get him there, he's not listening, he's not interested, he won't come to church, etc. But each of them in their own way carried a corner. Each one of them persisted. They didn't give up. And eventually, because of them - I got there.

Since becoming a Christian, I've had many experiences of encountering considerable challenges and seeming setbacks when trying to reach others for Christ. So much so that at times I honestly thought, this is just never going to happen - yet eventually, it did. A member of my family lives in the south of England. We maintained regular phone contact but only managed to visit each other once or twice a year. I have always been very open with her about my faith, and we spoke many times over the phone, and during visits about God's love for her and her need to accept Christ. This went on for twenty years, yes - twenty long years - with absolutely no evidence of her having any interest whatsoever. Like everyone else in life, she encountered problems and difficulties at times, and I always did what I could to be there for her.

There were times when a particular problem she struggled with really broke my heart because I knew if she had Christ in her life, everything would be so different for her. Just like the friends carrying the man on the stretcher, my wife and I did our best to support her through a number of these difficult times, always in the hope that she would see her need to accept Jesus. Just like the four friends, we just couldn't get her there. We tried everything. But we never gave up. I don't mean we never gave up on her; of course, family members should never do that, and we certainly never would. I mean that in the face of many failed attempts and disappointments over twenty years and, of course, a great deal of prayer, to get her to see her need for Christ in her life, we persisted in "carrying her" - in love, support, and prayer. Believing that some how we would eventually breakthrough. And break-through we did. Wonderfully, dramatically and very powerfully. When I say, "we did," I mean that's precisely what happened. One evening a number of years ago she phoned me.

The recurrent problem she'd had for several years had grown worse. This time when she phoned, she admitted she needed help. That was the first time she had acknowledged there was an actual problem. I knew that was the turning point for her. There has to be a turning point for each one of us. So long as we think we are ok, we won't seek God's help. It sometimes takes a crisis to make us face reality, and this was her reality check. So, after twenty long years of being carried in love and prayer, she was finally willing to acknowledge her need and accept help. Against seemingly insurmountable odds, over a very long period that could have caused us to give up, like the four friends, we simply didn't. Despite all the obstacles and failed attempts, we got there. By we, I mean she and us. We got there together. The remarkable thing is that though my wife and I immediately traveled to England and spent several days with her, during which time she went to church with us - nothing happened. She felt nothing and said she would never go to a church again. It was a very lively Pentecostal church service, and to put it in her own words, she thought everyone there was crazy.

It was a few weeks after we had returned home that she phoned us. She told us she had inexplicably felt the urge to return to the church on her own on two occasions. On the second occasion, she had a dramatic encounter with God and was converted on the spot, whilst sitting alone in the congregation.

Furthermore, she was instantly and permanently delivered from the problem that had previously afflicted her. And that deliverance was permanent.

What she described she experienced in that church service was truly remarkable. She said it was if an invisible hand had gone into her chest, taken out her heart, and put in a new one.

I remember being stunned by the similarity of that description of her experience with the words in Ezekiel 11:19-20 "I will give them one heart, and I will put a new spirit within them, and take the stony heart out of their flesh, and give them a heart of flesh, that they may walk in My statutes and keep My judgments and do them; and they shall be My people, and I will be their God."

She remains an exceptionally bright and dynamic Christian to this day and has led many of her friends to Jesus. As well as being a tremendous support and encouragement to me.

On another occasion and again over many years, the husband of one of my wife's cousins persistently claimed he had no interest in God. And, he would stress, no need for him. He admitted that he was impressed with our lifestyle because we seemed happy and content, but mainly because we always seemed to have folks around for meals and there was always lots going on in our house. He was very cynical, and his view was that some people needed religion as a crutch. Despite all that, we just kept on praying for him and 'carrying him' in friendship and through conversations about what he referred to as religion. Interestingly it was always him who raised the subject.

One evening I had to drop something off at his house and once again he wanted to talk. This time he had lots of questions, and I sensed that something had changed with him. He seemed more earnest and less cynical, and, at his insistence, our conversation lasted several hours (and umpteen cups of coffee.) As it was getting late, I suggested we could talk again soon. To my surprise, he suggested I visit the following evening. I called at his house the next day at around 7 pm. By 10 pm, we were still talking, and I felt exhausted. He was very sincere and had so many questions but was reluctant to open up to the gospel. I felt it wasn't right to try to convince or persuade him so I, suggested we call it a night. Although I'd shared many scriptures with him over the two evenings, I left him with a final bible verse. It was from the book of Revelation chapter three, where Jesus says, "Behold I stand at the door and knock, if any man will hear my voice, open the door and let me in, I will come in and eat with him and he with me." We then called it a night.

Several days later, I drove past him in the street. Because of the traffic, it wasn't possible to stop but just by the expression on his face I knew something had happened to him. I said to my wife when I got home: That man has had an encounter with God. Two days later, on a Sunday morning, my doorbell rang. There he was on the doorstep. A visibly changed man. He had peace written all over him. Once in the kitchen, he produced a small bible from his jacket pocket, which he had bought days earlier. He told me that after I had left his house on the second night of our discussions, he had gone to bed thinking about the last verse I had left him with. He said that after an hour, he got out of bed, got onto his knees, and prayed for the first time in his life. He was about forty years old at the time. He told me that he simply prayed, "God, I don't know if you are there, but if it's true that if I open the door of my heart that Christ will come in, then I open the door." That was it. He said he immediately felt flooded with something he had never felt before; he felt flooded with love. In an instant, he knew God was real, that God loved him, and that God had met with him. Whilst still on his knees, he said he "saw a vision of praying hands." Quite literally, two hands with palms facing in a gesture of prayer, and he heard the words "healing hands." He bought a bible, and upon reading, he was being led to scriptures all about healing, which he was keen to share with me. The tables had turned, quite literally overnight. Here was a forty-year-old cynical man who all his adult life had endless questions and a very skewed view of Christianity. As a brand new born again Christian, following his marvellous encounter with God, he was now teaching me from the bible. What a breakthrough. I had carried him onto the roof. And he had broken through to where Jesus was.

More recently, when I was employed as a local government officer, I was asked to provide a secure contact for a man who was in a drug rehabilitation centre in England during a visit to his family in Aberdeen. Because he was on parole, he was required to report to an official in the area he was visiting. I agreed to be that contact. The liaison staff in England told me that this man had attended church a couple of times whilst in rehab and that he was interested in finding out more about Christianity. They asked that I might recommend a local church he could attend during his visit. I met with him the day after he arrived in Aberdeen, and we talked over lunch. His name was Peter, and he had an extensive record as a drug user and dealer.

We established the protocol for his visit, and I advised him about churches in his area. He then began to ask me about my faith and my experience of salvation. We talked for an hour or so, and I said I had to get back to my office. He was feeling very anxious as he was due to see his family that night for the first time in years because of the damage his drug use had caused, and it became apparent that he needed some assurance. We went to my office to talk some more over coffee. An hour turned into two, and I said I had to get on with some work and set an appointment to meet up the following week. He told me that he really just needed to talk a little more about

Christianity then he very plainly asked how to get saved. This was once again pretty unconventional stuff. I was a senior manager, in my office with a parolee from another part of the UK, who I had never met before. My desk was piled high with work, and I had urgent calls to make. I had recommended churches to this man to attend, but he wanted to get saved - Now! So I took him through some scriptures and explained the need to repent and accept Christ as Saviour. He stressed that he wanted to do this and had been wanting to for some time but didn't know how. So I said OK, let's pray. He asked, "Shouldn't I get on my knees to pray?"

I replied that he should if that's what he wanted to do. He did and got onto his knees in the middle of my office. I naturally felt obliged to join him. He prayed very purposely and sincerely, accepting Jesus as Lord and Saviour, then very cheerfully left my office, saying he felt that a great weight had been taken off his shoulders.

As it transpired, we didn't need to meet again during his visit to Aberdeen. Staff from the rehab phoned sometime later to tell me the reconciliation with his family had gone very well and that he had returned to the unit as planned. I heard nothing further for about two months when I was in contact with the rehab on an unrelated matter, and I asked how Peter was. I didn't inform the staff of his decision for Christ as that is a private matter but what they told me was very concerning. They said that after returning from his Aberdeen visit that he was extremely happy and settled, but in recent weeks he had begun to revert to his old behaviour, wanting to go out drinking and being abusive to staff. Naturally, I was saddened and disappointed. I sought the Lord about it, and a few weeks later, I felt him say that Peter needed a 'second touch.'

Theologically, I don't truly understand what that means. I do know that when healing a certain blind man, Jesus had to pray for him twice before he could see clearly. That is the word that God gave me for this situation. It would be several months before I would be in the city where the rehab was, but I was determined to visit Peter. I phoned in advance and spoke to him briefly. He agreed to me visiting but was not too enthusiastic. When we met, Peter was flat in mood and didn't seem at all keen to see me. It made me feel as if I was a bit of a nuisance; after all, I didn't know this person. I did feel strongly in the Lord to 'carry' this situation, to carry Peter just a little bit further. To carry him that extra mile. After all, like the lame man on the stretcher, he couldn't do it himself.

To put it another way, I was 'on the roof,' and I wasn't giving up on him now. I asked him how he was and what had happened after he prayed in my office to receive

Christ. He told me he had felt really good for a week or so, but then his old feelings started to come back. He had then decided that his experience when he prayed couldn't have been real. We talked that through a bit, but it was mostly me who did the talking. Peter seemed indifferent, and I had a strong sense he didn't want me there. That made my next task even more difficult. God had told me Peter needed a second touch. Even with all my experience as a believer, I wasn't sure quite what that meant.

So how was *he* supposed even to begin to know what it was all about? But here we go, let's break through the barriers, let's push on despite the obstacles, despite the tangible resistance. "Peter - God, has told me you need a second touch, can I pray for you?" He replied - "If you think it'll make any difference." So I did. There and then, in that fairly unwelcoming atmosphere. I obediently prayed that God would give him a second touch. Peter was unmoved. I invited him to call me anytime and then left. I heard nothing further for several months; then, I learned that a week or so after my visit, Peter had attended a local church and had responded to an altar call. He went on to join that church and serve in the worship team. He abandoned his former life, married a girl he met in church, had children, and started what was to become a successful business. About three years after my visit, he phoned me to say he was doing great and to thank me for my support. Some hard work, some burden-bearing, inconvenience, anxiety, resistance, obstacles? Yes, all of these. But I simply persisted, with simple faith, availability, and persistence. Peter had many people around him, supporting him and carrying him on his way to finding Christ. I was just one of them. All that I did was carry my corner, go the distance, be radical, and simply not give up. It's always worth it because it can very often lead to a breakthrough.

Moving on from personal experiences of playing our part in bringing others to Christ, let's consider the example of the four friends, and the man on the stretcher, in relation to how that applies to the function of the local church. The local expression of the work of the church is described within scripture as the ministry of the body of Christ.

The New Testament model is very clear. Each one of us who is saved has received spiritual gifts from God through the indwelling Holy Spirit. These can also be referred to as spiritual abilities or talents.

These gifts are given to each person so that they are used to serve and support the other members of the body of Christ, which is the expression and outworking of the local church. It is made abundantly clear in scripture that we are each to submit to the headship of Christ, who is the head of the church so that he can place and position us within his church so that we each use those gifts to effectively play our specific part in the work of ministry. The work of ministry is twofold: To build up and encourage our fellow believers. And to reach out to those around us who don't yet know Christ.

All of which essentially amounts to - Teamwork. The four men carrying the lame man on the stretcher is a simple yet profound illustration of that. When a person gets converted and thereby becomes a member of the spiritual body of Christ, namely, the church - that is just the start of their journey. They then need to be supported, encouraged, loved, helped, taught, and discipled. They have a long road ahead of them, and they simply cannot make it alone. Neither are they supposed to or required to. That is simply not God's plan or design. God's design is that new Christians are incorporated into a strong local community of believers. A community represented by local church fellowships who work together as teams.

It might help to think about it this way: If a newly saved person begins to attend your church, depending on what kind of person they are or the life they are living, they will invariably need some degree of support, some greater than others. If providing that support fell on one member of your church, it would become too demanding. If it was shared by two church members, it would be half as demanding. If it was shared equally between four members, that extra responsibility would be even more manageable. There needs to be a clear understanding on the part of every church member that responsibilities should be evenly shared—not left to the leaders or only those who are willing to serve in this way.

Additionally, believers need to learn to understand and be aware of what their spiritual gifts/talents are so that they can use them for the benefit of others. That said, the greatest gift that every believer has - is love. And even if we don't know or understand what our "gifts" are, we can all reach out in compassion and love towards others. When I was a teenager, I worked a summer season on the docks at a Channel Island port. It was at a time when the trade unions were particularly strong, and due to strict union rules, when cars were offloaded from ships, the operation had to involve four dockers. Individual cars were mounted on large pallets. Each pallet had a large iron eye bolt on each of the four corners and a giant crane using four steel cables, each with an iron hook on the end and linked into the eye bolt, lowered the car on the pallet onto the quayside. The union rules dictated that each hook had to be removed by an individual docker.

It took four dockers to do the job. One for each corner. If one docker had a tea break or was absent for any other reason, the others weren't allowed to unlink his hook. When one man was missing the entire operation ground to a halt. The rule was one man, one corner, one hook. I know this is a fairly crude analogy, but I think it makes a valid point. Due to a lack of basic understanding, very many Christians simply are not manning their corner. They are not attending to their "hook." The wonderful and simple truth of the matter is that in many ways, that is all that's required of us. To be at our designated station. To provide practical service, friendship, fellowship, encouragement, and support and also, ideally, to exercise our spiritual gifts. Thereby actively playing our part in the work of the great commission and also contributing to what should be the amazingly diverse work and ministry of the body of Christ.

Returning now to the situation on the roof of the house that Jesus was in. The four friends had a dilemma. Having failed to gain entry to the house by conventional means, they had clambered to the roof, only to find it was covered. I can't imagine what they expected to find, as I assume that most roofs would be covered. Perhaps it was a section of the roof which could be opened depending on weather conditions. If so, its likely it could only be opened from the inside. That being the case, they couldn't open it anyway. Yet another obstacle, another disappointment, another discouragement. They could have thought, why aren't things working out for us, why is it all so difficult. Let's just pack it in. We've tried everything. Surely if God was with us? Or - we could just break open the roof? Yes, it's someone's property. The homeowner might not be too pleased. It might get us into trouble. But our friend on the stretcher is worth it. He only has one hope. And that hope is Jesus. We've already come this far. There's no going back now. Let's just do it! So "they uncovered the roof where he (Jesus) was. So, when they had broken through, they let down the bed on which the paralytic was lying."

Now *that's* radical!

Can you imagine just how awkward it would be to try to manhandle a man on a stretcher, horizontally, through a broken-up roof, down into a room full of people? How ridiculous that must have looked. How embarrassed the man (who I imagine must have been tied to the stretcher to prevent him falling out), must have been as he hung suspended between the hole in the roof, which his friends had just vandalised and the crowd of people in the room below. Just to make matters worse, we learn from the details in the story that the crowd in the room included scribes - religious leaders who were quick to criticize even the slightest indiscretion, never mind a lame man, crudely tied to some kind of bed, breaking in through the roof and suspended in mid-air. Talk about upsetting religious traditions, protocol, and norms!

But what was Jesus' response? It says that when he "saw their faith," he said to the sick man, "son, your sins are forgiven." This just simply staggers me. When he saw "their" faith, that is, not the lame man's faith but the faith of his four friends who had carried him and got him there. I think it's safe to say it was their faith Jesus was referring to because he spoke directly to the sick man telling him his sins were forgiven. Incidentally, as we read the rest of this in the Bible we discover that the man was also immediately healed because he began to walk in full view of everyone there.

So Jesus commended and honoured the faith of the four friends. He commended their obvious joint efforts. Efforts which required remarkable - teamwork. Teamwork without which it would be quite simply impossible for them to accomplish their task. Teamwork, without which they could not even have begun such a daunting challenge. By commending the faith of the four friends, Jesus was commending their persistence. He was commending their innovation. He was commending them for taking risks, and for being so radical in their evangelism in bringing someone to him. But above all, I believe he commended and honoured them for the care, compassion, and love that motivated and drove them.

A final observation from this great picture just has to be mentioned. Those in the room with Jesus, into which the four friends so unceremoniously lowered the man in the bed, included scribes, who, not unlike the Pharisees, were religious leaders, who loved to debate scripture and biblical laws and traditions and criticise anyone who didn't meet their criteria. That's about all they ever did, which is why Jesus was often openly very critical of them. Astonishingly, we see that despite this amazing scenario occurring before their eyes, they chose to focus on the words that Jesus used when he spoke to the man on the stretcher. Rather than being glad about this man being brought to Jesus and that he was also miraculously healed, all they wanted to do was gripe about religious terminology. Their hard-hearted religious blindness prevented them from celebrating the miracle that had taken place. Or to offer their appreciation and admiration to the four friends who had made such dedicated efforts.

In closing, then we see two kinds of people represented here: The first kind are those who like to sit inside a house with Jesus but just *talking* about religion. The second kind is those who take action and who are prepared to do whatever it takes to get someone to meet Jesus. (The comparison to church life here is fairly obvious). I'm sure Jesus must have been relieved, having listened to the 'religious experts' deliberating for who knows how long, when four dedicated believers quite literally broke into the meeting. Probably doing some things the wrong way - but for the right reasons!

I suppose we could each ask ourselves at this point which of these two kinds of people we identify most with - the ones on the roof or the ones in the room?

And finally - if you find that your style of radical evangelism upsets the rules - well, they were most probably man-made anyway.

I'm sure you'll agree that there is so very much we can learn from this wonderful picture.

Thomas Malone

Chapter Six

The Greatest Miracle

(Jesus' revelation to Nicodemus)

Gospel of John Chapter 3:1-21

[1]*There was a man of the Pharisees named Nicodemus, a ruler of the Jews.* [2]*This man came to Jesus by night and said to Him, "Rabbi, we know that You are a teacher come from God; for no one can do these signs that You do unless God is with him."*

[3]*Jesus answered and said to him, "Most assuredly, I say to you, unless one is born again, he cannot see the kingdom of God."* [4]*Nicodemus said to Him, "How can a man be born when he is old? Can he enter a second time into his mother's womb and be born?"*

[5]*Jesus answered, "Most assuredly, I say to you, unless one is born of water and the Spirit, he cannot enter the kingdom of God.* [6]*That which is born of the flesh is flesh, and that which is born of the Spirit is spirit.* [7]*Do not marvel that I said to you, 'You must be born again.'* [8]*The wind blows where it wishes, and you hear the sound of it, but cannot tell where it comes from and where it goes. So is everyone who is born of the Spirit."*

[9]*Nicodemus answered and said to Him, "How can these things be?"*

[10]*Jesus answered and said to him, "Are you the teacher of Israel, and do not know these things?* [11]*Most assuredly, I say to you, We speak what We know and testify what We have seen, and you do not receive*

Our witness. [12]If I have told you earthly things and you do not believe, how will you believe if I tell you heavenly things?

[13]No one has ascended to heaven but He who came down from heaven, that is, the Son of Man who is in heaven. [14]And as Moses lifted up the serpent in the wilderness, even so must the Son of Man be lifted up, [15]that whoever believes in Him should not perish but have eternal life. [16]For God so loved the world that He gave His only begotten Son, that whoever believes in Him should not perish but have everlasting life. [17]For God did not send His Son into the world to condemn the world, but that the world through Him might be saved.

[18]"He who believes in Him is not condemned; but he who does not believe is condemned already, because he has not believed in the name of the only begotten Son of God. [19]And this is the condemnation, that the light has come into the world, and men loved darkness rather than light, because their deeds were evil. [20]For everyone practicing evil hates the light and does not come to the light, lest his deeds should be exposed. [21]But he who does the truth comes to the light, that his deeds may be clearly seen, that they have been done in God."

The subject of this particular picture is, I believe, without doubt, the most amazing, unique, and astonishing truth available to humanity.

A truth so simple yet so profound, so readily available and accessible to all, yet unknown and lost to so many.

It is also a truth that is fundamental and pivotal to understanding the depths of the entire bible from Genesis to Revelation. A truth that transcends all of men's efforts, religious or otherwise, including those who identify as a Christian, whatever shade of doctrine, to interpret the bible by their own efforts. It is this truth that is presented within the frame of Jesus' brief conversation with a man called Nicodemus.

The "frame" of this picture is Jesus's conversation with Nicodemus. The picture within the frame is the subject they spoke about.

A man called Nicodemus approached Jesus and said to him, "Rabbi, we know you are a teacher who has come from God because no man can do the miracles that you do unless God is with him." The bible says that Jesus "answered him." However, Nicodemus hadn't asked a question. Why should Jesus answer him when he hadn't asked a question? Here's another example of the fact that God doesn't necessarily communicate the way we might expect him to. We think one way, he thinks another. We have one agenda; he might have another. We think we need something, but he already knows what we really need. And he takes the opportunity to demonstrate that to us when we speak to him, that is - when we pray. I think that when we pray about something we need or want an answer to, that is, when we initiate contact with God, we are then actively 'listening' because we are then hoping for an answer to our prayer.

While we are in the listening (or expecting) mode, God uses that opportunity to tell us what 'he' wants to say. He uses that opportunity to speak into our lives things that he, as our Heavenly Father, knows that we need to hear. And it is very often not the thing we have asked for in prayer. Why do I think that's the case? I think it's because he knows that we generally don't pray enough. That we generally don't spend enough time in his presence listening to him. As such, he doesn't always get the opportunity to teach us things because we are too preoccupied and busy. Too preoccupied and busy with life. And for the Christian today, perhaps often too preoccupied and busy attending an array of church meetings.

When we pray or ask God for something or for guidance or direction, we expect that he will engage us at that point, on that subject or even at that level. He sometimes quite simply just doesn't. We may then feel that God hasn't answered our prayer, or even that he is isn't listening. If you are a Christian, you will be familiar with those parts of Jesus' teaching when he tells us what *not* to pray for or ask for. He says, "seek not what you should eat, what you shall drink or how you shall be clothed." Why? Because he says, "your Heavenly Father (already) knows that you have need of those things." He goes on to say, "but seek (ask for) first (things that relate to) the kingdom of God." *(Bible Ref: Matthew 6:31-33)*

So, we might pray, asking God for things that he is already going to provide. So, he doesn't engage us at that level. He takes the opportunity whilst we are making an effort to ask and listen, to talk to us about something else, something 'spiritual,' something that he wants us to understand. Something that he *does* want to give us and that he does want us to receive. Let's put it this way, if, as a parent, your small child asked you - Mummy/Daddy, will you please feed me today? What would you do? I'm quite certain you would simply ignore what they said and talk to them about something else. You would talk to them out of your heart of love for them. You would talk to them about things that mattered, things that make them happy, that make them feel secure, that help them grow and develop. You would tell them things *you* wanted to tell them, things you know they need to know. I'm fairly sure you wouldn't have a conversation about whether or not you were going to feed them that day. So, you will not have answered their question, just like when we think God hasn't answered our prayers.

I think this was the case with Nicodemus and Jesus. Nicodemus wanted to talk to Jesus about miracles, or "signs". It becomes immediately evident that Jesus has no intention of picking up on that subject with Nicodemus and that he was going to talk to him about something else entirely. Indeed he proceeded to do just that. There are a few facts that we need to know about Nicodemus, and those facts are contained within this brief encounter. Within the text, it says that Nicodemus was a ruler of the Jews. Jesus referred to him as being a master of Israel. And Nicodemus refers to himself as being old. Nicodemus was a Pharisee and was knowledgeable in all things concerning the law of Moses, the teachings of the prophets, and the rest of Old Testament scriptures. He was an expert in the Jewish religion and a highly esteemed leader within the community. He was a very pious man, a very religious man, and to all intents and purposes, a good and moral person.

Nicodemus had evidently either seen or heard about some of the miracles Jesus had performed, and I suspect he wanted to talk to Jesus about them. Perhaps to learn more about them, or perhaps to debate points of Jewish tradition or doctrine.

But Jesus didn't want to talk to Nicodemus about the miracles he had performed. He wanted to talk to him about "The Greatest Miracle." A miracle that surpasses all other miracles. A miracle that surpassed all miracles then. A miracle that has surpassed all miracles since. A miracle that still surpasses all miracles now. And a miracle that will surpass all other miracles until such times that Jesus comes again to this earth.

Nicodemus said to Jesus, "Rabbi, we know you are a teacher who has come from God because no man can do the miracles that you do except God be with him." In response, Jesus appears to have ignored what Nicodemus had said and instead simply stated: "Indeed I say unto you, Except a man be born again he cannot see the kingdom of God."

Nicodemus, this great, learned, and seasoned Jewish religious leader, obviously shocked at what Jesus had said, responded to his remarkable statement by asking a very natural and practical question. "How can a man be born when he is old, can he enter the second time into his mother's womb and be born?" No doubt and quite understandably, as that is the only frame of reference he had, Nicodemus was mentally picturing the process of a baby being born and is perplexed that this remarkable person standing before him is telling him this has to happen again. That is, it has to happen again - to him!

Surely this must be one of the most peculiar exchanges of dialogue between two people ever recorded. Just think about it - "born again!" "Enter a second time into a mother's womb!" Astonishing. Yet - much of the gospel hangs on this statement made by Jesus. And that being the case, a true understanding of the entire bible - Old and New Testament, hangs on it.

Once again, Jesus doesn't answer Nicodemus's question. Instead, he then states, "Except a man be born of water and of the spirit, he cannot enter the kingdom of God."

I think it's very significant that Jesus chose to so clearly and so graphically expound this particular truth to Nicodemus rather than anyone else at the time. Why? Because Nicodemus, like so many religious people then, since and now, may know a lot of religious stuff, but they can still completely miss the point. They miss that which is of most importance. In knowing lots of 'stuff,' they then can't see the wood for the trees. There are also those who, like Nicodemus, may have spent an entire lifetime in religious service, religious study, or both, yet fail to grasp the simple truth.

Someone once said - If your compass is faulty, then your whole direction will be wrong

It also emphasises that learning by itself, even much learning, doesn't promise to lead a person to the truth. It can make a person very knowledgable or very religious if religion is what they are studying or practicing. It doesn't mean they know the truth. I think that Jesus, specifically choosing to reveal this to Nicodemus, also serves to emphasise that even though a religious leader may be very knowledgable in their field and have vast experience or even be of great age, it still doesn't follow that they have an edge on truth. The very same can be said of religious qualifications, titles, and high office within church life and throughout church organizations. The fact that someone may have attained any of these doesn't and shouldn't automatically imply they are equipped to lead others spiritually. Nicodemus met all these criteria but still needed to be taught the truth. It surely follows that any church leader can only take their members as far as they have themselves gone. They can only teach what they understand. And they can only shed light to the extent that they have it. Or don't have it, as the case may be.

Contained within this narrative, is a very clear message and to take it a bit further, a very clear warning, not to put all of one's store in a spiritual or religious leader.

Jesus then proceeds to expand on what he said. He added, "that which is born by natural means is natural, but that which is born by spiritual means is spiritual." In other words, a person is born physically of human parents but is born spiritually of the Spirit. Spiritual birth is something totally separate and completely different. Not as Nicodemus had pondered, i.e., to be born naturally from his mother a second time.

Jesus continued, "Don't be amazed at what I'm telling you, you must be born again." He immediately went on to explain to Nicodemus that when a person is born again, which he then also refers to as being "born by the spirit" that it's like when the wind blows, that you can't see it, but you can hear it. And that you can't tell where the wind is coming from or where it's going.

But Nicodemus was still perplexed and asked Jesus, "How can these things be?" I think another way to phrase his question might be - How does that work?

Jesus then said to Nicodemus, "You are a master in Israel, you should know these things." He was reproving Nicodemus and telling him off. He was saying, you've been learning the Jews religion all your life, you hold the highest office in your line of work, and you've been teaching and leading others, how then could you then have missed this? He no doubt was also implying; just what *have* you been teaching people all these years?" A thought perhaps for any Christian leaders or ministers reading this? Elsewhere in scripture, Jesus said, "If a blind man leads another blind man, shall they not both fall into a ditch?" He was referring to spiritual blindness and posing the question that if a person was blind to spiritual truth, as apparently Nicodemus was, how could they expect to lead others spiritually? A person may have a title; they may have a degree in divinity or religious studies. They may even have a doctorate. They may have all the associated religious garb and hold high office in a church, but if they aren't "born again" of God's Spirit, then they are in precisely the same position as Nicodemus.

Should any church leader reading this find that offensive, they need to consider just who set this criteria. It was Jesus.

He told Nicodemus, a veteran and highly esteemed religious leader that - unless he was born again by the Spirit, he could neither see or enter the kingdom of God. So, if any person can neither see or enter the kingdom of God - it stands to reason that they are not qualified to teach about it or lead others into it. Yes, they can teach religion, but religion in itself doesn't convey and explain the message of the kingdom of God. And that is the message that Jesus taught and preached.

So, using the very same analogy that Jesus himself used; As the only way to enter the natural world is to be quite literally born into it, so the only way to enter the kingdom of God is also to be born into it. The 'birthing' principles are precisely the same; it's just that the 'realms' are different. One is physical, tangible and visible. The other is spiritual, intangible, and invisible. Love as an emotion or a feeling, is the most deeply, passionately and strongly felt of all emotions, and is in itself, intangible and invisible. It is nevertheless very physical, tangible, and visible in its effect.

Similarly, the very air that we breathe is invisible. But life would not exist without it. Atoms are invisible, yet they are the very building blocks of all physical, tangible, and visible matter.

It is a remarkable illustration of the blindness of the human heart and mind that when it comes to matters relating to God and indeed all things spiritual that so many people say the cannot and will not believe in something they cannot see.

All the while, the fact is that without the things that we cannot see, the things that we *can* see wouldn't exist. Life wouldn't exist. *We* wouldn't exist.

Jesus stated elsewhere in scripture that people's hearts had grown very hard, and because of this, even though they have eyes, they cannot see, and even though they have ears, they cannot hear. He then announced that the only solution was for people to come to him "be converted, and he would heal them." In other words, their capacity to see and hear spiritual things was faulty; it had shut down. That was precisely the condition of Nicodemus. He knew a lot but he couldn't see spiritual things. That's why he couldn't understand about being born again. The only aspect of anything being born that he could understand had to be the physical kind. Why? Because, despite all his knowledge, all his experience, and all his religious understanding, he was spiritually both deaf and blind. I believe Jesus chose to have this particular conversation with Nicodemus to demonstrate to everyone who would read about it thereafter, (including you and me) that it simply does not count that a person might be profoundly religious or even have a lifetime of experience and service in religious matters. And that applies to all and any religions, not just Judaism or Christianity. A person may even have a string of qualifications or titles in a particular field of theology or divinity, yet they are still spiritually blind unless they get converted. Given that this would apply to those who are perceived to be the most religiously qualified, by virtue of their position in a religious hierarchy, just like Nicodemus, then it must surely also apply to everyone else. Including those who have absolutely no interest in God.

The 'pass mark' - is to be converted. To be converted means to be spiritually healed by Jesus. Being spiritually healed by Jesus results in a person, any person, religious or not, being born again. And Jesus said - you *must* be born again. You *have to be* born again. As we were all born naturally by natural means, to become a natural - living person. So, God says we have to be born spiritually to become a spiritual - living person.

Perhaps in speaking to Jesus, Nicodemus was hoping to see Jesus perform a miracle. Or perhaps he was hoping to learn more about how miracles work. Maybe he wanted to know what conditions had to be met for a miracle to occur. Or it could be he just wanted to add personally meeting Jesus to his religious list of things to do. We don't know. What I believe we do know, is that Jesus was not interested in giving Nicodemus anything that Nicodemus thought he needed.

Jesus was intent on giving Nicodemus what Jesus knew he needed. Jesus knew that giving Nicodemus what Nicodemus wanted would not benefit him.

More knowledge wouldn't benefit him. More information wouldn't benefit him. Yet another religious experience wouldn't benefit him. Jesus knew something about Nicodemus, and he knows something about absolutely everyone, and it's this:

What we all need is LIFE - Spiritual Life. A spiritual life that only he can give. A spiritual life that every one of us needs to receive - and can only receive - from HIM.

Jesus was saying to Nicodemus - stop looking and start living. He was saying - you've come to the right place and you've come to the right person because *only I* can give you what you're looking for. It is only me who knows what you need. Jesus was saying to Nicodemus - let's not talk about miracles. He was saying - I want to *give you* a miracle. I want to perform that miracle here and now. I want to perform that miracle for you right now. I want to perform that miracle - *in you* - right now.

I want to open your blind eyes and open your deaf ears so that you will be able to see. So you will be able to see not only natural, physical reality. Not only the natural and physical world. But so you can also see spiritual reality, the spiritual world - the kingdom of God. And that in seeing it you will be able to enter it, live in it and be part of it.

Another reason I think that Jesus specifically chose to speak to Nicodemus on this subject as a religious leader of considerable standing, was that other people in the community will have undoubtedly looked to him for guidance, for religious guidance, and spiritual guidance. The very same applies today all around the world. People generally look to religious leaders of whatever religion or denomination when seeking religious guidance or in living out their faith. That said, religion can for very many people in today's society, sometimes prove to be a very confusing subject.

After all there are different religions and different forms of expression, as well as varying and often conflicting interpretations of teaching and traditions within those religions. As such, it can all get very complicated and confusing. All of which is perfectly understandable and not helped by some of the archaic and, at times, convoluted religious jargon and terminology used within some churches and other faith communities.

I believe that's why Jesus especially said to Nicodemus what he did. He was saying, Nicodemus, let's cut to the chase, you need to be born again. Nicodemus, all that you know and all the good things you do as part of your religion is good and commendable, but you need to be born again. Nicodemus, if you want to lead others to the truth, you will never do it by trying to explain everything you know to them. It's too complicated. It has taken you years, even a lifetime, to understand it.

Jesus was telling Nicodemus that people aren't looking for religion, they're looking for meaning, they're looking for a better life, they're looking for help, they're looking for reality, they're looking for God.

I believe that Jesus was very intentionally cutting through religion. He was cutting through layer upon layer of historic doctrine and tradition. He was cutting through the fog of man-made mystery that envelops and enshrouds the actual truth. He was dispelling the religious hierarchy that so often unwittingly hinders rather than helps people find God. He was saying, Nicodemus, when all is said and done, you - and everyone else - quite simply need to be born again.

Jesus had no intention of adding even more layers to Nicodemus' extensive library of doctrine. He was not going to add yet more religious terminology to his vocabulary.

Jesus' use of the term "born again" was very intentional for the reasons I have already suggested. But Nicodemus' response about entering in a second time to his mother's womb also greatly helps us understand this terminology in another very significant way. Jesus went on to explain to him that that which is born by natural means is natural but that which is born by spiritual means is spiritual. The keyword here is "born." To be born. Born naturally and born spiritually. They are both used in the same context to mean precisely the same thing. Just one is natural and the other spiritual. When we were each born 'naturally,' we had no understanding of what was going on. We didn't have the faculties to know what was happening. And even if at the time our mother tried to explain to us (sounds ridiculous, I know) well, it's just too ridiculous and impossible even to consider it. Yet here we are. We exist.

Furthermore, being born required absolutely no effort on our part. We didn't plan it. We had no part in preparing for it. We weren't required to learn, know, or understand anything about it. And yet it happened. We didn't know where we came from or where we were going. But other people did. Our parents understood what was happening. It was them that did all the planning. It was they who gave us life. And in due course, we grew to understand it.

Jesus explained to Nicodemus, that's just what it's like when a person is born again, he said it's like the wind, you don't know where it's coming from, you don't know where it's going - but there it is.

Just like a newborn baby, you simply cannot comprehend it, but it's real. And it creates life.

Now, if a person were never born 'naturally,' they would simply not exist. There would be no existence of that physical person. It's how we all start. There is no other way. There is no other start. Either it's born, or it isn't. We don't need all of Nicodemus' vast religious knowledge or experience to understand that. We can all simply humanly relate to the profound simplicity of being born. Because it happened to each one of us - that's why we exist. Plain and simple!

To be born is to start from the beginning. To start from scratch. To start from zero. Growth, awareness, learning, knowledge, and understanding all come later. Later - not before. Being born, knowing nothing and understanding nothing, and yet being immediately aware of new life. That is precisely the same when a person is born again. Yet so much of what we would call Christian religious traditions, systems, hierarchies, religious life, structures, and religious doctrines, would have us believe that a person has to know certain things already. That they need to understand certain things, or attain some level of goodness, in order to be a Christian.

This then creates layers of complexity that confuse and obscure the wonderful simplicity as to how we can each reconnect to God, which, from a biblical perspective, is what becoming a Christian means.

That is what Jesus wanted to impact Nicodemus with. Nicodemus merely wanted to *talk* about miracles, to *know about* miracles. Jesus wanted to demonstrate to him that he could personally *experience* a miracle, a miracle within his own heart and within his own life - the greatest of miracles.

You don't enter spiritual life at an academic level. Neither do you enter it at a religious level. Jesus explained to Nicodemus- you enter it via birthing. You have to be born into it. To enter into a relationship with God- you have to be born into it. To enter into the kingdom of God - you have to be born into it. To enter into the family of God - you have to be born into it. To enter into the church - you have to be born into it.

A great deal of confusion, misunderstanding and, to be blunt - ignorance, could be avoided if this core teaching of Jesus was better understood. Across the world there are many and varied definitions of what it means to be a Christian. Some 'Christian' denominations teach that if a baby or small child is christened or baptised that they become a Christian at that point. Others teach that if a child's parents identify as Christian, that means their children are also Christians. Certain denominations teach that joining their membership role makes a person a Christian. Some people believe that by identifying with biblical principles and morals makes them Christian. While others think that occasional church attendance is all that's required. There is also the misconception that living in what is perceived as being a Christian country somehow confers Christianity on its citizens.

However, the biblical definition of what it means to be a Christian (a follower of Christ) is very clear in the actual teaching of Jesus himself - who is, after all, the one who Christians seek to worship, serve and obey.

There is also a fundamental problem concerning how Christianity is perceived nowadays by many people. On the one hand, people associate Christianity with religious public figures and institutions in the same way that Nicodemus was perceived in his time and culture. He and his fellow Pharisees will have looked a certain way, dressed a certain way, sometimes wearing religious robes and hats, etc. They will also have held services and ceremonies in religious buildings that will have followed a certain form of worship. Just like many of the more formal churches today, with services and ceremonies held in traditional buildings with steeples and spires and so on. Many of those buildings represent great historical and religious heritage, and they continue to be vibrant centres of worship and a host of great works throughout communities. However, to non-Christians, they can seem to be outdated and outmoded. Whilst this is very often just not the case at all, to non-Christians, they may nevertheless appear not to be very relevant to contemporary 21st-century culture.

Then there is the issue, as mentioned earlier, of the many perceived definitions of what a Christian is and what being a Christian means. So, what is its true definition? What does it mean to be a Christian, and how can a person become one? The good news is, those are precisely the issues dealt with in Jesus' brief encounter with Nicodemus.

To summarise what we have already learned about that brief encounter, Jesus demonstrated to Nicodemus the following:

- *Your religious traditions don't count.*

- *Your religious titles don't count.*

- *All your religious knowledge doesn't count.*

- *Your religious doctrines don't count.*

- *Your religious interests don't count.*

- *Your religious studies don't count.*

- *Your religious efforts don't count.*

- *Your religious enthusiasm doesn't count.*

- *Your religious experience doesn't count.*

- *Your religious 'goodness' doesn't count.*

- *Your religious ceremonies don't count.*

- *Your attendance at religious services doesn't count.*

- *Your religious buildings don't count.*

It's not that all of those things aren't of significance or value. It's not that they aren't worthy, commendable, and even honourable. Of course, they all have their own merits. It's just that absolutely none of those things are either necessary or required for a person - absolutely any person and every person -to become a follower of Jesus Christ.

Christianity, according to what Jesus himself taught, and what the rest of the New Testament confirms, clarifies and builds upon, represents a brand new start, a completely new beginning, a clean slate, a second chance, a brand new life - and a whole lot more.

How often have we heard people say: If only I had another shot at life. If only I could have a second chance. Oh, that I could have my life to live over again! No doubt we have all had such thoughts from time to time.

Perhaps there is something innate within every person, something deep down, hidden in the sleeping recesses of every mortal soul, that somehow knows that this is a possibility. And that is why there is the occasional flicker, just a flicker, of faint light, a faint light from a distant 'somewhere,' but we just don't know where - and then it's gone—gone in the busyness of life. Gone in the demands of life. Gone in the myriad distractions of life. Gone in the daily pursuit of life itself. Gone - even though without it, though we don't know it, the very things in life we are pursuing every day and the very life we are living, is limited and restricted in so very many ways compared to the life we could have.

Why do I say that, and upon what basis can I make such a statement? Firstly, I say it because the bible tells us that without Christ in our lives, without being born again of the Spirit - we are only partly alive. We are only physically and naturally alive. But our spiritual life is dead. It does not yet exist. It has not yet been born. To live fully - as God intended, we must be both physically and spiritually alive. We were made physically alive the day we were born. We are similarly made spiritually alive the day we are born again. When a person is born again, they are then *both* physically *and* spiritually alive. Secondly, I say it because spiritual life opens a whole new dimension for us. When a person is born again, they feel different; they see things differently, they see the world differently, they see themselves and others in a different light. Their moral values and their priorities change. Why is this? It's because when a person is born again - the Spirit of God enters their life. When we are born naturally, we are born with 'human nature.' But when a person is born again - they are born with a spiritual nature. And that spiritual nature is God's nature. As I have already mentioned, there are great similarities concerning natural birth and spiritual birth. A newborn baby knows and understands absolutely nothing. It does however know it's alive, simply because it's, well, 'alive.'

Similarly, when a person is born again spiritually, just like a newborn baby, they know and understand very little initially, but they do know they are now spiritually alive - because the new life of the Spirit of God within them 'exists.' And they know it. They can feel it. They have become alive but in a different way, in a new way.

Before a child is born, it cannot hear its mother's voice; neither is it aware of her presence. But from the moment it's born, it is immediately aware, and it can suddenly hear the voice of its mother.

It's the very same when a person is born again, born of God's Spirit. That person suddenly and immediately senses a new presence and 'hears' a new voice - the voice of God the Father. I can imagine the thoughts just now of some readers of this book who might be thinking - but that's preposterous, how can a baby 'know,' and how can we know that a baby knows and hears the moment they are born? The answer is quite simple, we know because every one of us has been through that process - and we are here to prove it. We are each the evidence. We are each evidence of the miracle of birth.

We understood absolutely nothing at the time, but now we are grown; it's all very clear and quite understandable. It is only when our natural faculties have developed that we can look back and understand these things. Similarly, when being born again, it is also only when our spiritual faculties have developed that we can understand it from a spiritual perspective.

Nicodemus' response to Jesus, telling him he needed to be born again, was one of incredulity. He said to Jesus - But how can these things be? Jesus' response truly opens the door to our understanding of spiritual matters because in saying what he did, he appealed to Nicodemus's understanding of natural things, in order to explain to him why he had difficulty understanding spiritual things. Jesus answered: "If I told you about natural things, you wouldn't believe me. How then will you manage to understand spiritual things?" Jesus was, in essence, saying to Nicodemus, you are so far removed in your intellectual sophistication and worldly wisdom that you have forgotten even the wonder of natural life, the miracle of life itself, and even the very source of life.

If your heart is so hardened to natural things, how are you going to manage to grasp basic spiritual truth? He was saying; you don't even really understand how you got here in the first place, how you came to exist naturally, but if you will consider that, you will better understand how a person can be born spiritually. He was saying, as all-natural human life comes from God, so does spiritual life. However, people forget that. They forget it was God who made them. They forget they belong to God. They forget they are accountable to God. And over time, they rebel against God. They rebel against the knowledge of God. Then in time, they deny there is a God. And finally, they insist there is no God.

Despite all the evidence of the world around them. Despite all the evidence of everything that absolutely everyone can physically see, taste, touch, hear and feel, despite the very miracle of being born. Despite the very wonder and miracle of the very life we all live and enjoy - we deny there is a God.

Jesus' reply to Nicodemus wasn't just for him; it was for everyone. It was for each one of us. It was for you, and it was for me.

Jesus was explaining that people's hearts have become so rebellious and hardened against God that they, like Nicodemus, had become both deaf and blind to the truth. And if they have become so hardened to natural truth, which they could see, feel, touch and hear, how could they possibly even begin to understand with their natural faculties, with their natural intellect, with their natural reasoning, spiritual things, for which there is no physical evidence?

That, Jesus, told Nicodemus, is why you have to be born again. You have to start over again. You have to start from scratch. You have to start from zero. You have to come into God's spiritual world (kingdom) the same way you came into the physical world. You have to be born into it. Understanding nothing, knowing nothing, and having no part in the process. That process is entirely in God's hands and under his control. Just like when a baby is born. Think about it this way; when a baby is born, it comes into the world naked, bringing nothing with it. It is wholly reliant on others. The life it has is a gift from others. It is a gift, humanly speaking, from its parents. It is fundamentally a gift from God. Parents, by themselves, can't create life. Life is created through them, not by them. God is the Creator of life, and he is the giver of life. Each of us didn't do anything to be born. We didn't contribute in any way whatsoever. We did absolutely nothing to earn the gift of life. We couldn't do anything to earn the gift of life. That is simply not within our power. It is God's domain. And it is God's domain alone.

Similarly, to be born again, we cannot create that new spiritual life ourselves. We can contribute nothing to it. We can't earn it by religious practice or good behaviour. Like a naked newborn baby, we can bring nothing of ourselves to it.

We have no influence over it. In the same way that natural, human life is a gift to us from God, so also is spiritual life. It also is a gift from God. There is only one thing that we can do - and that is to accept it, receive it. A gift, any gift, in the hands of a giver, intended to be given to someone as a gesture of love and friendship - simply has to be received by the person it is offered to. If, however, a person doesn't acknowledge the gift or refuses to accept it - it stands to reason that they can't benefit from it, enjoy it and perhaps not even ever know what it was.

Many people will be familiar with the quote from Jesus: "Suffer little children to come unto me and forbid them not, for of such is the kingdom of heaven." A common understanding of that verse is that it suggests children are innocent and unblamable and pleasing to God. Whilst that might have some merit, the actual meaning is that people who are like children and are prepared to become 'childlike' are the kind of people who will enter the kingdom of God. Jesus qualifies this by also saying: "Except you be converted and become as little children you shall not enter the kingdom of heaven." There needs to be some simple clarification at this point, and it's this: The terms kingdom of God and kingdom of heaven are interchangeable and have the very same meaning. They both refer to the kingdom of God here on earth and here and now. Neither of those terms refers to a celestial 'heaven,' a place where people may go when they die. Whilst there is such a place, when Jesus was talking to Nicodemus, he was referring to a spiritual realm, one which coexists here and now, with our 'natural' earthly realm.

But remember, Jesus told Nicodemus that unless a person is born again, they cannot 'see' the kingdom of God (the spiritual realm). That a person cannot 'see' the kingdom of God might also be interpreted as 'perceive' or be aware of.

It might be helpful for the reader to consider a few natural facts at this point whilst we are considering a spiritual kingdom that exists right now but that we cannot see. We can't see the air that envelopes our planet, but without it, nothing would live or grow, and absolutely no one would survive for more than a few minutes. We also can't see atoms yet they are the building blocks of the visible physical world and of life itself. Even with our advanced technology, astronomers can still only glimpse a tiny fraction of the universe. The rest of it is quite simply invisible to our eyes. But it would be absurd to say that because we can't see it (let alone begin to understand it) that it isn't there.

We can't see the sun at night, but that doesn't mean it doesn't exist. Similarly, we can't see the stars during the day, but we know they are there. Yet when it comes to God and spiritual matters relating to God, so many people claim - I'll believe if I see it. And, if I can't see it, it can't exist.

The reason a small child cries so bitterly when they realise that Mum or Dad isn't in the room is because in the child's, as yet undeveloped mind, it thinks that if it doesn't 'see' its parent that they no longer exist. They don't yet understand that the parent does exist but just somewhere else without being seen at that particular time and place by the child. Equally, if a man is at work and his wife was at home, he can't see her, and neither can anyone else in his workplace. When he tells his colleagues he has a wife, it would be ridiculous for them to say - well, we can't see her, so she obviously doesn't exist. She simply cannot be real because we can't see her. Because, as adults, we have grown physiologically to understand about time and space and coexistence. This is precisely one of the many 'natural' things that we take for granted as we mature physically and intellectually. But we take them for granted to the extent that we grow hard and even cynical to the wonder of it all.

That is why, because when we have grown hard and cynical to the wonder of natural things, we fail to grasp the concept of things at a higher spiritual level.

That is what Jesus was referring to when he said to Nicodemus, "If I were to speak of natural things to you, you would not believe me, how then will you understand spiritual things." As we considered briefly earlier, spiritual things are not so out of the ordinary if we were to appreciate better and indeed wonder in amazement at creation and the natural world around us.

So we see that Jesus said that to enter the kingdom of God, a person must become like a small child, a baby. But he then also said that a person needs to be 'converted.' So what does that mean? To answer that question, we need to briefly consider more of what Jesus taught concerning this. Jesus taught mostly in parables. A parable is a spiritual truth but presented in a natural context or by practical illustration. It's presented in a natural context because that's how people understand things. So by teaching spiritual truth by practical illustration, the listener has something to hold on to, something to compare it with. Here are just a few examples of Jesus' parables:

"Therefore hear the parable of the sower: When anyone hears the word of the kingdom, and does not understand it, then the wicked one comes and snatches away what was sown in his heart. This is he who received seed by the wayside. But he who received the seed on stony places, this is he who hears the word and immediately receives it with joy; yet he has no root in himself, but endures only for a while. For when tribulation or persecution arises because of the word, immediately he stumbles. Now he who received seed among the thorns is he who hears the word, and the cares of this world and the deceitfulness of riches choke the word, and he becomes unfruitful. But he who received seed on the good ground is he who hears the word and understands it, who indeed bears fruit and produces: some a hundredfold, some sixty, some thirty."

The seed represents the word of God being preached and the different soil conditions as representing the various conditions of people's hearts and their willingness or unwillingness to hear and receive it.

"Again, the kingdom of heaven is like treasure hidden in a field, which a man found and hid; and for joy over it he goes and sells all that he has and buys that field."

This parable is an illustration of someone who experiences the wonder of discovering God and all the 'treasures' that this new life has to offer. So much so that they then invest all of their life into discovering more from then on.

"What do you think? If a man has a hundred sheep, and one of them goes astray, does he not leave the ninety-nine and go to the mountains to seek the one that is straying? And if he should find it, assuredly, I say to you, he rejoices more over that sheep than over the ninety-nine that did not go astray."

The spiritual meaning of this parable is to illustrate how much God loves people and how he desires for everyone to be gathered into his care. *(Bible Ref: Matthew 13:18 / Matthew 13:44 / Matthew 18:12)*

So, on the subject of needing to be converted, this is what Jesus taught: He said that people's hearts had become hardened against spiritual matters and against God.

He said it was as if, even though people had eyes, they cannot see. And even though they have ears, they cannot hear.

So, though people can see natural things and hear natural sounds, they are blind to spiritual reality and deaf to spiritual sound. Deaf to spiritual sound refers to being deaf to the voice of God. And being deaf to the meaning of the spoken word of God and being able to hear what it has to say to us. Jesus taught that people's natural condition is that they need to be spiritually healed. Furthermore, he taught that it is only he that can heal them. Then, once he has healed them spiritually, they are, in effect, 'converted.' Converted from being spiritually deaf and blind to be fully aware of spiritual reality. That is, becoming fully aware of the existence and reality of God. To be converted is to be born again. Born again, from being dead to spiritual matters, to becoming alive to them.

So, to summarise: Jesus interchangeably used the terms, born again, healed, and converted.

Reflecting on this and all that we have looked at so far in this chapter - a person is spiritually healed and converted - when they are born again. When a baby is born, it is born with the faculties to see, hear, and feel naturally and physically. When a person is born again, they are born with the faculties to see, hear, and feel spiritually. A baby is born possessing human nature. Similarly, when a person is born again, they are born again, possessing spiritual nature. And as a baby, then gradually grows and matures in its understanding of the physical world. So, a person who is born again then gradually grows and matures in their understanding of the spiritual world. And it is this spiritual world that Jesus refers to as the kingdom of God. And those two realms, or 'kingdoms' - co-exist.

So, Jesus told Nicodemus - "You must be born again." Nicodemus responded by simply asking, - how? Yes, he expanded upon his question by adding the supposition - can a man enter a second time into his mother's womb? But leaving that aside as we have already dealt with it, we are still left with the question: How? Just how can a person be born again?

Jesus went on to answer that question as he continued to talk to Nicodemus, uttering probably the most commonly known verse in the whole of the New Testament. He said, "For God so loved the world that he gave his only begotten Son (meaning born of a woman) that whosoever believes in him should not perish but have everlasting life." *(Bible Ref: John 3:16)*

Jesus went on to explain that he came into this world to draw all people to himself, and to God. He further explained that he didn't come to judge or condemn people, but rather that he came to draw them to the light. He explained further that if people chose not to come to the light, it was because they preferred to live in darkness.

That darkness being the darkness of living in ignorance of God - and *preferring* to remain spiritually, deaf and blind.

This explanation given by Jesus is core to understanding the rest of the New Testament.

Why? Because it makes it very clear that how we each live is a matter of personal choice. How we each relate to God - is a personal choice. And especially, how we each respond to the proclamation of the gospel, is very much a personal choice.

So just what is "the gospel?" The word gospel means - 'good news!' And the good news is that God sent Jesus into the world to show us the way back to Himself. Not only to show us the way through everything that he said and taught but also to make that way possible by giving his life on the cross as an atonement for our sins. Throughout the bible, it is very clearly taught that even without the teachings of Jesus and the proclamation of the gospel, we all intuitively *know* there is a God. We know because of all the evidence of the created world around us. And we know because we are created beings. However, so often, we *choose* to ignore it, avoid it and then deny it. Whilst in his conversation with Nicodemus, Jesus stressed that he did not come into the world to condemn it, but rather to 'save' it, he explained that people are already condemned.

Condemned may seem a very harsh term, particularly in our increasingly liberal and secularized culture. Nevertheless, condemned means to have been judged, found guilty, and sentenced. But why are people condemned? The Bible explains it this way: Firstly, we are guilty of ignoring and even denying the God of creation. The very God who created us. Secondly, when the gospel is declared to us - explaining that we are guilty of ignoring God but offering a way to put that right - we 'choose' to also ignore and deny that. We, in effect, condemn ourselves. We condemn ourselves by taking the position that - so there is a God, or, even if there is a God - I don't need him, I don't want him, I don't want to know what he has to say, I don't want a relationship with him. And I'm not going to accept what he has to say.

I'll live life my way. I'll live my life on my terms, and I'll do whatever I want to do. Jesus explained to Nicodemus that 'the condemnation' was that light (meaning himself) has come into the world, but people refused to come to the light because they prefer to live in darkness. Yet, many people who have no time for God and who, as such, reject him, will often take the position that they will turn to him when they need to or when they are old.

Others take the view that 'if' there is life after death, that God will accept them anyway because he is a God of love. Firstly, both those perspectives are entirely contrary to what the bible (the actual book about God) has to say on the matter. That is why people should take the time to search out and learn the truth.

Secondly, using a natural analogy to illustrate a spiritual point, let me put it this way; Would a married man or woman, who wilfully chose to ignore and neglect their spouse throughout their lifetime and also deny they had any responsibility towards them, then expect that 'relationship' to work out alright in the end. And for that shunned and rejected person to love them anyway? Of course they wouldn't. The outcome would be inevitable. But whose fault would it be? Would it be the fault of the person who was denied, shunned, and neglected? Of course it wouldn't. The blame for that failed relationship and the tragic outcome would sit squarely on the shoulders of the person who was neglectful, irresponsible, and rejecting.

Their ultimate condemnation concerning that failed relationship would be entirely of their own making.

So it is with God. He is there. He is always there. His offer of love is always there. His offer of relationship is always there. His offer of knowledge about him is always there. It is us who choose to ignore it. It is us who choose to neglect it. It is us who choose when God prompts us at various points in our lives, as well as through the presentation of the gospel message, to reject him. We simply cannot say when all is said and done; I didn't know, I didn't understand, I never heard. No, because we are each given a lifetime to know, to understand, to reach out, to seek, to learn, and to discover. It is us who *choose* not to. God has done his part. He has done everything he can do. As Creator, he has created everything around us for us to see and experience. As Redeemer, he sent Jesus to be our Saviour. You might be reading this right now and thinking, well, I didn't know, I've never heard, I don't understand. Well, if you have read this far in this chapter alone - *you do now!* You now know as much about the way to salvation as Nicodemus did. You now know what Jesus told Nicodemus. And what Jesus had to say to Nicodemus then, is precisely the same as he has to say to each one of us now. So, what are you now personally prepared to do about it?

The greatest miracle, the greatest of all miracles is this: it is a miracle of a changed life. A life that is changed through an encounter with Jesus. It is the miracle of new birth. A new spiritual birth. A new spiritual birth that is available to anyone and everyone. Yes, absolutely anyone and everyone, anywhere, everywhere, and at any time.

A new birth. A new nature. A new beginning. A clean slate. A new relationship with Almighty God. A new revelation of life, its meaning, its purpose, its origins, and its destiny. A new life, where a person's heart is changed, where their blind eyes and deaf ears are opened. Jesus performed many and varied miracles; some no doubt that Nicodemus was referring to. However, each of those miracles only had short term or temporary effects. The miracles of water into wine and the feeding of the five thousand were only time and place-specific. Those same people (in the natural sense) would be hungry and thirsty again the next day. Lepers were healed, the lame walked, but they would one day die. So their miracle was temporary. It was for this life only. Even Lazarus, who Jesus raised from the dead, would still one day die. However, the miracle of the new birth - lasts forever. Yes, it is eternal. You see, Nicodemus, even with all his religious understanding, was still focussing on temporary, or temporal matters. Jesus immediately wanted to take him higher, to take him further, much further.

For the true Christian, a person who has been born again, eternal life doesn't begin when they die. No, eternal life starts the very moment they accept Christ into their lives. When a person accepts Christ into their life, they receive the Spirit of God. And the Spirit of God is eternal. It is only people, human beings, who have a time-limited life. It is human nature that has a time-limited life. Remember what Jesus told Nicodemus: "For God so loved the world, that he gave his only Son, that whosoever believes in him should not perish (die) but have - everlasting (eternal) life." Jesus also said: "If a person believes in me, they shall never die, and even if they die, they shall live again because I will raise them up on the last day."

And the truly amazing and wonderful thing is this: God's offer of a new life 'now' and eternal life in the future is completely and unconditionally available and freely offered to absolutely everyone. Yes, each one of us. Regardless of age, religion or indeed, the absence of it, or lifestyle or gender, past or present wrongs or wrongdoing. It is a free gift. The bible says this: "For the wages (the consequences) of sin (a life wilfully lived without God) is death but the gift of God is eternal life - through Jesus Christ the Lord." *(Bible Ref: Romans 6:23)*

So there we have it; "The Greatest Miracle." It is a miracle that becomes a reality for many people from every background, culture, society, and nationality all around the world every day as they respond to the eternal message of the bible. It is a miracle that, once experienced, encompasses, contains, and reveals the very source, meaning, and truth about life itself. And which also dispels ignorance, spiritual blindness, spiritual bondage, falsehood, myth, and deception. Yet, tragically, it is something that so very many people still remain completely unaware of.

Thomas Malone

Conclusion

That's it then. That is my offering. Those are my six 'pictures.' My "Apples of Gold." I hope you enjoyed reading them, or better still, 'viewing' them. I would like to think that, like any picture or painting of interest, you might return to them from time to time to take another look. And that in doing so, you will perhaps see something, some small but significant detail you hadn't noticed the first time. I think that each picture, whilst presented together, also stand out alone and distinct. They can be revisited individually and in any order.

Hopefully, also, the Christian reader will pick up on the many doctrinal threads and themes that are woven throughout each picture. I could have included reams of related bible chapter and verse but have generally preferred to let the pictures themselves tell the story

- In Chapter One, the disciples 'walked out' their life with Jesus.
- In Chapter Two, they 'poured out' the new wine.
- In Chapter Three, they 'launched out' into a life of adventure and service.
- In Chapter Four, they 'dished out' the 'Bread of Life' to others.
- In Chapter Five, they 'carried out' their duties as disciples of Jesus.

I passionately believe that the New Testament profoundly demonstrates that 'teamwork' involving the absolute necessity of the active and dedicated contribution of every believer, *is* the New Testament plan and design that God has instituted for the healthy, balanced and optimum effectiveness of his church. I use the term teamwork with confidence because that ultimately is what it is. I am, of course, referring to the true function and nature of the body of Christ - the church - as clearly detailed and outlined in scripture. No more so than in Paul's teaching in First Corinthians chapter twelve, Romans, chapter twelve, and Ephesians chapter four. Particularly beautifully and succinctly summarised in Ephesians 4:11-16, which I will now sign off with:

"And He Himself gave some to be apostles, some prophets, some evangelists, and some pastors and teachers, for the equipping of the saints for the work of ministry, for the edifying of the body of Christ, till we all come to the unity of the faith and of the knowledge of the Son

of God, to a perfect man, to the measure of the stature of the fullness of Christ; that we should no longer be children, tossed to and fro and carried about with every wind of doctrine, by the trickery of men, in the cunning craftiness of deceitful plotting, but, speaking the truth in love, may grow up in all things into Him who is the head—Christ— from whom the whole body, joined and knit together by that which every joint supplies, according to the effective working by which every part does its share, causes growth of the body for the edifying of itself in love."

End

Tom Malone is available for book interviews and personal appearances. For more information contact:

Tom Malone
C/O Advantage Books
P.O. Box 160847
Altamonte Springs, FL 32716
info@advbooks.com

To purchase additional copies of Apples of Gold visit our bookstore website at:
www.advbookstore.com

Other books by Tom Malone:

What Are Your Children Watching?
ISBN:9781528947053
Austin Macauley Publishers (2019)

Longwood, Florida, USA
"we bring dreams to life"™
www.advbookstore.com